MAKE YOUR OWN

JEWELLERY

MAKE YOUR OWN

JEWELLERY

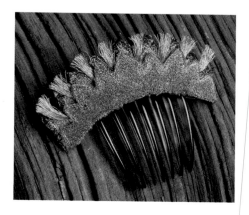

More than 100 ideas for
creating stunning pieces
from everyday materials

EDITED BY Ann Kay

LORENZ BOOKS

This edition is published by Lorenz Books

Lorenz Books is an imprint of Anness Publishing Ltd
Hermes House, 88–89 Blackfriars Road, London SE1 8HA
tel. 020 7401 2077; fax 020 7633 9499
www.lorenzbooks.com; info@anness.com

UK agent: The Manning Partnership Ltd, 6 The Old Dairy,
Melcombe Road, Bath BA2 3LR; tel. 01225 478444
fax 01225 478440; sales@manning-partnership.co.uk

UK distributor: Grantham Book Services Ltd, Isaac Newton Way,
Alma Park Industrial Estate, Grantham, Lincs NG31 9SD
tel. 01476 541080; fax 01476 541061; orders@gbs.tbs-ltd.co.uk

North American agent/distributor: National Book Network,
4501 Forbes Boulevard, Suite 200, Lanham, MD 20706
tel. 301 459 3366; fax 301 429 5746; www.nbnbooks.com

Australian agent/distributor: Pan Macmillan Australia,
Level 18, St Martins Tower, 31 Market St, Sydney, NSW 2000
tel. 1300 135 113; fax 1300 135 103
customer.service@macmillan.com.au

New Zealand agent/distributor: David Bateman Ltd,
30 Tarndale Grove, Off Bush Road, Albany, Auckland
tel. (09) 415 7664; fax (09) 415 8892

A CIP catalogue record for this book is available from the
British Library.

Publisher Joanna Lorenz
Editorial Director Helen Sudell
Project Editor Ann Kay
Copy-editor Beverley Jollands
Designer Design Principals
Editorial Reader Rosanna Fairhead
Production Controller Wendy Lawson

Main image on front cover: Fishy Cufflinks project, p140

10 9 8 7 6 5 4 3 2 1

The publishers have made every effort to ensure that all
instructions contained within this book are accurate but
cannot accept liability for any resulting injury, damage or
loss to persons or property, however it may arise. Readers are
reminded that due care and suitable precautions (such as
wearing goggles or gloves, for example) must be taken when
undertaking certain craft projects. Seek expert advice about
this if in any doubt.

Contents

Introduction	6
FABRIC AND LEATHER	**8**
Feltwork Materials	10
Feltwork Equipment	11
Feltwork Techniques	12
Ribbonwork Materials	13
Ribbonwork Techniques	14
Ragwork Materials and Equipment	16
Ragwork Techniques	17
Leatherwork Materials and Equipment	18
Leatherwork Techniques	19
Feltwork Projects	20
Ribbonwork Projects	30
Ragwork Projects	38
Leatherwork Projects	47
MACHINE EMBROIDERY	**50**
Materials and Equipment	52
Techniques	53
Projects	56

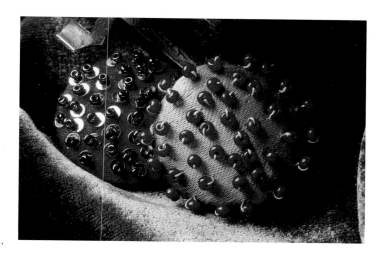

BEADS AND SHELLS 76

Beadwork Materials and Equipment 78
Shellwork Materials and Equipment 80
Bead and Shellwork Techniques 82

Beadwork Projects 84

Shellwork Projects 107

ENAMELLING AND METALWORK 112

Enamelling Materials 114
Enamelling Equipment 115
Enamelling Techniques 116
Sheet Metal and Wirework Materials 120
Sheet Metal and Wirework Equipment 121
Sheet Metal and Wirework Techniques 122

Enamelling Projects 124

Metalwork Projects 162

PAPER, CARD AND WOOD 170

Paper and Card Materials 172
Paper and Card Equipment 173
Paper and Card Techniques 174
Woodworking Materials and Equipment 177
Woodworking Techniques 178

Paper and Card Projects 179

Woodwork Projects 191

CLAY, MOSAICS AND GLASS 198

Claywork Materials 200
Claywork Equipment 201
Polymer Clay Techniques 202
Modelling Clay Techniques 205
Mosaic Materials 206
Mosaic Equipment 207
Mosaic Techniques 208
Glassworking Materials 210
Glassworking Equipment 211
Glassworking Techniques 212

Clay Projects 214

Mosaic Projects 234

Glass Projects 238

TEMPLATES 242

Index 250
Acknowledgements 255

Introduction

Everyone loves jewellery, whether to wear or to give, and it seems to fill a basic human need. Many of the oldest artefacts found by archaeologists have been personal ornaments, and all over the world jewellery has always been just as significant for its meaning as for its intrinsic beauty and worth. It's a universal symbol of wealth, power, love and desire. Yet the word "jewel" is derived from a Latin word for a plaything, and jewellery can certainly also be a source of pleasure and amusement. While you might keep family heirlooms such as pearls and diamonds in the bank, the pieces you choose to wear every day have a different kind of value – they're a daily delight and a perfect way to express your personality, especially if you've made them yourself.

This book takes a sideways look at the art of making jewellery and concentrates on pieces that don't require specialist skills or costly raw materials. While it does include some beautiful, delicate pieces in silver, enamel and beadwork, there are also surprising and original ideas for turning mundane ingredients such as clay, paper and felt into characterful jewellery, transformed by clever ways with paint and gilding. You can even discover how to create glittering filigree confections using your sewing machine.

Beautiful photographs of around 100 lovely pieces will inspire you, whether you follow the detailed step-by-step instructions to reproduce the designs exactly or use the techniques describe

to develop your own variations. The projects range from simple brooches and necklaces that total beginners could manage to sophisticated etching and enamelling techniques: just follow the pliers symbols and tackle the simplest examples of each technique first. As well as the jewellery itself – from earrings and necklaces to hair decorations and cufflinks – you'll also find a selection of beautiful boxes. Any of these would make an attractive addition to your dressing table, while one of the little trinket boxes would be a wonderful way to present a handmade piece of jewellery as a gift.

Jewellery Fittings

To make your own jewellery, you need a variety of fittings, such as necklace clasps, brooch pins, chains, metal pendant "blanks" that you can infill with enamel, and earring wires. The term "findings" is the name given to the many different parts used to fasten or link jewellery. The best-known findings include jump rings (the small metal rings used in all kinds of ways to link different parts of jewellery items – for example, to join the end of a string of beads to a clasp) and butterfly backs (for holding studs in place in pierced ears).

If you become very adept at metalwork, you might choose to make most of these kinds of things yourself, but in the meantime certain craft stores, and some jewellery stores, sell an enormous range of fittings to make jewellery-making really easy. You can also obtain fittings from the many companies selling them to the trade; most of these operate mail order schemes and have easily accessible websites.

Fabric and Leather

Textiles of all kinds offer endless scope for creating original necklaces, brooches and hair decorations, and you may find you already have nearly everything you need to explore these ideas: scraps of pretty fabrics or leather, shimmering ribbons and a scattering of beads. Really unusual pieces can be created using the crafts of feltwork, ribbonwork, ragwork and leatherwork, producing exciting, textural works of wearable art.

Made by turning wool fibres into solid fabric, felt is an ideal jewellery material as it is lightweight and can be created in any number of lovely colours. Wool can also be mixed with fibres such as silk and mohair.

Feltwork Materials

Carded sliver

This wool is commercially sorted into fibres of the same length, bleached and carded into a long rope ready for spinning or felting. You can buy it pre-dyed or dye it yourself.

Commercial felt

Felt pieces are now available from general craft suppliers in a wide range of colours.

Dye

Acid dyes – so-called because an acid such as vinegar must be added to the dye bath – are ideal for wool. They need very hot water to work well, but give good colourfast results.

Felteen

This is a clear fabric stiffener commercially used in the making of felt hats. PVA glue diluted with water can also be used to stiffen felt, but will leave a surface sheen.

Glass beads

Beads in a wide range of sizes and shapes can be stitched directly on to felt items as decoration.

Jewellery findings

Standard findings are easily attached to felt pieces, using either thread or epoxy glue. Use nylon-coated jewellery wire to thread felt beads.

Thread

Ordinary sewing thread can be used in a sewing machine to create embossed lines or relief effects on thin felt. As well as being used for embroidered decoration, metallic thread can be trapped under a thin web of fibres and felted into the fabric.

Uncarded fleece

Fleece needs to be cleaned, dyed and carded, but it gives greater scope for experimentation than prepared sliver. Felt is best made from wool with a staple or fibre length of 2.5–5cm/1–2in: longer fibres will tangle. The ideal wool for feltmaking is Merino.

Much of the equipment needed for feltwork can be improvised; felt made from carded sliver requires no specialist items. The most important thing is a cloth or mat in which to roll the felt.

Feltwork Equipment

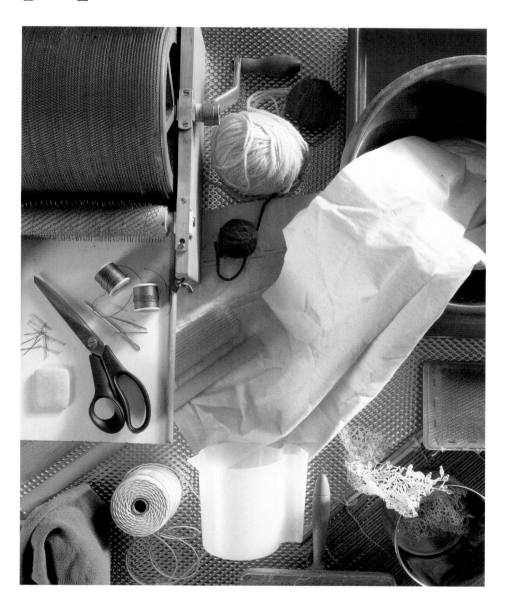

Bamboo mat

Rolling the fleece on a bamboo or sea-grass beach mat increases friction and speeds the felting process.

Craft (utility) knife

A very sharp blade is essential for cutting cleanly through felt balls.

Drum carder

This will card a large amount of wool quickly, but is an expensive piece of equipment, only really necessary if you do a lot of feltmaking.

Hand carders

Once you get into the rhythm, wool can be carded by hand quite quickly. If you have no carders, use pre-carded sliver, which can be teased open with your hands.

Needles

For sewing felt choose "straw" or "milliner's" needles, which are extra long with small eyes that do not create a bulge in the shank. A needle with a large eye and a sharp point is useful for threading felt balls and beads.

Scissors

To cut through felt smoothly scissors need to be really sharp. Dressmaker's shears are needed for cutting out flat pieces of felt, and small sharp-pointed scissors for embroidery and beadwork.

Soap flakes

All soap will make felt, but some kinds have properties less advantageous to the feltmaker. For example, washing powder is too harsh and hand soap washes out too quickly. Pure soap flakes are most suitable as they are very mild and easy to rinse out.

String

Any string that will not disintegrate in hot water or stain the wool when wet can be used to hold carded wool in hanks during the washing and dyeing processes. Cotton string is best as knots will not slip and it can be re-used many times.

The transformation of a mass of loose wool fibres into a solid piece of felt is a mysterious and intriguing process, as it requires only the action of heat, moisture and friction, aided by soap.

Feltwork Techniques

Making Felt Balls and Beads

A small ball will take about 20–30 minutes. When the wool is fully felted the ball will have shrunk considerably and will bounce if thrown hard on to a table.

1 Twist a length of carded wool into a tight ball. If the finished ball is to be cut in half, for example when making buttons or earrings, use several colours to achieve a marbled effect.

2 Cover the ball in another layer of carded wool, wrapping it around evenly. Keep the ball in your hand to stop it falling apart. Dip the ball in hot, soapy water, squeezing it to wet it through to the middle.

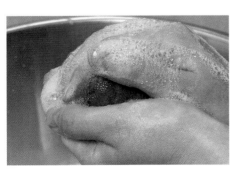

3 Roll the ball gently in your cupped hands. As the fibres begin to felt, increase the pressure steadily and dip the ball back in the water from time to time. When the wool has fully felted, rinse out the soap and leave to dry. The ball may be put in a spin drier or on a radiator to speed this up.

4 To make a bead of a different shape, such as an egg-shape, squeeze the ball into the form you need once the outer layer has hardened but while the core is still soft. Complete the bead as before, without losing the shape.

Dyeing Wool

The felt jewellery in this book has been made using carded sliver, which is wool that has been industrially cleaned and carded. This can be bought pre-dyed, or bleached ready for dyeing.

1 To dye fleece or wool sliver, follow the dye manufacturer's instructions to make up a dye bath of hot water and lower the wool into it.

2 Slowly bring the bath to the boil and allow to simmer for an hour. Do not stir or prod the wool, as this will cause felting. Allow the dye bath to cool before lifting out the wool and drying it in a warm airy place, away from direct heat.

Ribbons come in an appealing variety of colours and textures, from silks and velvets to glittering metallics and exotic patterns. Basic sewing equipment is all you need to transform them into exquisite ornaments.

Ribbonwork Materials

Ribbons

As ribbon weaving keeps pace with technology, an ever-wider range becomes available. The individual project will dictate the kind of ribbon you need, and your choice should depend not only on colour and pattern but on the finished effect you require. For example, a basic single-loop bow can be made from any type of ribbon and still look stunning, whereas more elaborate looped and gathered designs may demand soft satin or wire-edge ribbon to look really effective.

Woven-edge ribbons – These have selvedges down each side; they are often made to very high standards and are washable: each reel should carry full details of crease resistance and colour fastness. They are primarily intended for use on clothing and soft furnishings. A huge variety is available, including taffeta, moiré, woven checks, and single- or double-faced satin. High-quality embroidered ribbons can be expensive, but are effective in small amounts when used in jewellery-making. The narrowest widths of satin ribbon are suitable for threading beads. They can also be used for rich embroidery, or as delicate streamers to trim hair decorations.

Craft ribbons – These are purely decorative and offer many interesting surface weaves and a variety of wired edg-ings. A satin-stitched edge, often encasing a fine wire, is known as merrow edging. Wire-edge ribbons can be moulded into stable loops for creating bows and flowers.

Glue

PVA (white) glue can be used to fix your ribbon designs in place. A glue gun is not absolutely essential but makes it easier to apply glue with speed and accuracy.

Wire

If you are making stemmed ribbon roses as part of your jewellery design, then you will need florist's stub wire to maintain stiffness in the stems. Flexible florist's wire is wrapped around the base of the flower to secure the shape properly. Remember that you must avoid using scissors to cut the wire, however thin, as this will ruin the blades instantly – always use wire cutters.

With a little practice in manipulating ribbons into loops and bows, and a few basic sewing techniques, you can turn these simple strands of colour into exquisite artefacts.

Ribbonwork Techniques

Wire-edge Ribbon Rose

This quick and easy decoration is perfect for attaching to a hairslide (barrette) or brooch. For a medium-sized flower you need about 90cm/1 yd of 39mm/1½in ribbon. Artificial rose leaves can be added by binding them to the stem using green florist's tape (stem wrap).

1 Tie a knot in one end of the ribbon. From the other end, pull the wire from one side of the ribbon, creating gathers.

2 Using the knot to form the centre of the flower, wind the gathered edge around its base.

3 To add a stem, twist one end of a florist's stub wire around the base of the rose, then wrap the exposed ribbon wire around the top of the stem.

4 Tease the ungathered ribbon edge into petal shapes. Cover the wire stem with green florist's tape (stem wrap), adding artificial leaves if you wish.

Right: *The shading of ombré taffeta wire-edge ribbon contributes to the realistic appearance of these roses.*

Ribbon Bows

The classic hand-tied bow needs no stitching or wiring, but both can be used to produce a perfect bow that won't come undone.

Hand-tied Bow

1 Fold a length of wire-edge or traditional soft ribbon in half to find the centre point. Fold each half of the ribbon across the centre to make two loops and two tails. Hold the ribbon layers together securely and bind a piece of fine florist's wire tightly around the centre.

2 Conceal the florist's wire by wrapping a short piece of matching or contrasting ribbon around the centre of the bow. Secure it with either glue or a couple of small handstitches at the back. Trim the tails of the bow neatly if necessary and gently pull the bow loops and trimmed tails into the required shape.

Multi-loop Bow

1 Find the centre of a length of ribbon as before and fold the ribbon into the desired number of loops, making sure that you keep all the loops the same size and that you hold the centre of the bow firmly in place. There should be an even number of loops on each side of the centre.

2 Secure the mid-point of the folded loops and form the centre of the bow by binding with a length of fine florist's wire. Conceal the wire with a short piece of matching ribbon and glue or stitch it in place at the back. Trim the ribbon ends and tease out the loops attractively.

Ribbon Embroidery

Embroidering small-scale projects using narrow ribbon creates intricate textural effects.

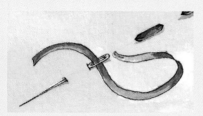

Running stitch is used both decoratively and to join or gather fabric. Pass the needle in and out, keeping the stitches small and even. Push the fabric along the thread to gather it.

For cross stitch, work a row of diagonal stitches from right to left, then complete the crosses by stitching from left to right.

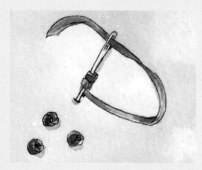

To make a French knot, bring the thread up through the fabric and twist the needle around the ribbon two or three times. Insert the needle just beside the point where it came up and pull the thread down through the twists to form a knot.

Since the essence of ragwork is its economical use of recycled fabrics, the materials and equipment needed are minimal. The most unlikely materials, even including plastic bags, can be used to great effect.

Ragwork Materials and Equipment

Adhesives

Latex carpet adhesive can be used to back finished pieces of ragwork. Use clear impact adhesive to attach backing fabric and strong epoxy resin glue to secure jewellery findings.

Fabrics

Cotton – Jersey fabrics, such as old T-shirts, fray very little and make excellent looped surfaces. Printed shirts and dresses are also ideal.
Nylon – Thin jersey (such as coloured tights) makes a fine-textured surface.

Felt

Black felt makes a smart backing fabric to finish pieces of jewellery such as brooches and earrings.

Hessian (burlap)

Old sacking was the traditional recycled foundation for hooked rag rugs but nowadays hessian, made from jute, can be bought by the metre or yard. It is strong and pliable and the threads open and close easily when hooking. It is available in different weights – 250g/9oz is perfect for ragwork.

Hook

A tapering, sharp-ended brass hook with a turned wooden handle is pushed through the hessian to make a large hole, through which the fabric is hooked. A large crochet hook can also be used to hook small pieces.

Hoop

Hessian needs to be stretched taut on a frame for ragwork; an embroidery hoop is suitable for small projects such as jewellery.

Plastic bags and foils

Strips of plastic sheet, such as carrier bags, can be used with or instead of fabrics. Add sparkle with foil-backed crisp (chip) packets and gift wrap.

Scissors

You need two pairs: sharp dressmaking shears for cutting fabrics and pile and another pair for paper, foil and plastic, as these will blunt the blades.

Sewing materials

Findings such as brooch backs and earring clips can be stitched to ragwork pieces, and backing fabric can be slip-stitched in place. Embroidery thread (floss) is used for decorative finishes.

Wire

Thin wire is useful to stiffen the ragwork for sculpted pieces.

All ragwork involves cutting fabric into strips but several techniques can be used to work them into the finished item. Use contrasting materials and surface treatments to create a wide range of textures.

Ragwork Techniques

Hooking   This is the commonest and most versatile technique, in which fabric strips are hooked through hessian (burlap). They can be left as a loop pile or sheared to create a cut pile surface. A combination of the two surfaces gives a sculpted, three-dimensional effect.

1 With the hessian in a frame, push in the hook and feed on a loop of fabric. Pull the hook back, bringing the end of the strip to the top. Push the hook back in 1–2 warp threads away and then feed a loop on to the hook as before.

2 Pull the hook back to make a fabric loop approximately 1cm/½in high. Repeat in order to create rows of loops to cover the hessian. When you reach the end of a strip, pull it through to the top. Trim to the same height as the loops.

3 To create a cut pile surface, pull the fabric through in loops as before but hook them to a height of approximately 2cm/¾in. When the area is filled, shear across the tops of the loops with a large pair of scissors.

Backing and Finishing   Once the ragwork is complete the edges of the hessian need to be neatened and the back covered. Backing jewellery pieces with a soft fabric such as felt will prevent the hessian irritating the skin.

1 Trim around the finished piece to leave a hessian border at least 2cm/¾in wide. Spread latex adhesive all over the back and leave to dry for 3–5 minutes, then fold in the edges.

2 Cut any excess hessian away at the corners to make the underside as flat as possible.

3 Cut a piece of felt slightly larger than the ragwork. Pin around the edge and slip-stitch in place, turning in the excess felt as you go.

Leather offers a distinctively unusual material for jewellery. Leatherwork is a skilled craft, but small-scale jewellery projects can be accomplished using little more than basic sewing materials and equipment.

Leatherwork Materials and Equipment

Adhesives

PVA (white) glue can be used to stick pieces of leather together if the surfaces are roughened to provide a key. Use epoxy resin glue to attach jewellery findings.

Leather

Hide can be bought by the full skin or in cut sections that are ideal for small projects. Skins are available natural or pre-dyed in a wide range of different finishes and colours, including metallics. Skiving leather is a natural undyed hide that has been pared down in order to make it thin enough for moulding.

Leather stain

Stains are water- or alcohol-based. Unlike dyes or paints, which colour the surface, stains penetrate the skin.

Felt-tipped pens

For small items, coloured decorations can easily be added to natural leather using permanent felt-tipped pens. Translucent pens allow the grain to show through the colour. Treat leather decorated in this way with beeswax before polishing it.

Needles

Leather needles – Embroidery needles may be sturdy enough for very fine skins, but leather needles are better able to pierce thicker hide.

Glover's needles – These have a three-sided point that acts as a cutting edge. They are available in a range of sizes.

Punch

A rotary leather punch is used to make holes, both decorative and functional. Choose a good-quality punch with replaceable cutting tubes.

Scissors, knives and shears

Special leather scissors are sturdy with rounded ends. Small shapes can be cut using a craft knife and cutting mat. Use pinking shears to add a decorative edging to lightweight leathers.

Sewing thread

Linen thread is used for most leatherwork, and is waxed to help it slip through the skin easily. Cotton thread may be strong enough for fine skins, and embroidery thread (floss) can be added for decoration.

It's a good idea to practise any techniques for shaping or decorating leather on scraps or offcuts of a similar colour and thickness before using them on your chosen piece of skin.

Leatherwork Techniques

Punching

A row of punched holes, perhaps combined with a pinked edge, makes an effective decoration for fine leather.

It's best to place a scrap piece of thick leather under the item you are punching to protect the cutting tubes. If you need to get to a point beyond the reach of the punch, try folding over or gathering the leather.

Moulding Leather

When dampened, vegetable-tanned, undyed leather can be moulded into shapes that it retains when dry.

Thick leather needs to be soaked to soften the fibres, but small thin pieces need only be moistened with a sponge and warm water. Press the leather into the desired shapes using your fingers.

Dyeing Leather

Protect the work surface and work in a well-ventilated area if you are using alcohol-based dye. The leather must first be cleaned so that it is completely free of grease, as this can resist the dye.

1 To clean the leather, make a solution of oxalic acid (5ml/1 tsp to 600ml/1 pint water) and rub over the surface using a soft cloth. Leave to dry. Dampen the leather with a sponge then apply the dye with a cloth, working over the surface in a circular motion.

2 It is easier to obtain an even colour if you apply several layers of dye. Apply polish to seal the surface and make the colour permanent.

This bright necklace is fun to wear and easy to make. The large beads are very light and will not weigh you down. Experiment with different shapes of beads, and try mixing colours to create a marbled effect.

Felt Bead Necklace

you will need

50g/2oz fleece, in carded slivers, in various colours

soap flakes

bowl

2 crimp beads

nylon-coated jewellery wire

necklace clasp

small pliers

large needle

1 Divide the fleece into bundles to make 19–21 beads, each containing two or three colours. Wind and twist each bundle into a tight ball, keeping it in your hand to stop it falling apart.

2 Dip each of the balls that you have just made in hot, soapy water. Now squeeze and roll each ball in your hands to felt the fibres until you can feel that the ball is hard all the way through. Rinse each bead under a hot tap then a cold one, and allow to dry. (A spin dryer will help speed up the drying process.)

3 Lay the beads out in the order in which you want to thread them. Thread a crimp bead on to the nylon-coated wire and then one half of the clasp. Turn the wire back through the crimp bead and crush the bead, using a small pair of pliers, to secure the wire.

4 Thread the wire on to a large needle then push this through all the beads to thread them on to the wire. Attach the other half of the necklace clasp as described in step 3.

Though this bracelet has a chunky look it is light and soft to wear. You can vary the end result by adding embroidery, sewing on beads or artificial flowers, or incorporating other yarns under the surface of the felt.

Felt Bracelet

you will need

40g/1½oz fleece in carded slivers, three colours

string

heavy weight

soap flakes

bowl

scissors

needle and matching sewing thread

1 Divide each length of fleece in half. Make the wool up into two plaits, each of the three colours, leaving two additional strands unplaited. Tie the two plaits and the two strands together at one end with string and attach the string to a heavy weight. Twist the plaits and strands tightly together and tie the other end of the twist securely with string.

2 Wet the wool thoroughly with hot, soapy water, keeping the plaits and strands in a twist. Rub the length of the fibres with plenty of soap, using one hand to keep the twist pulled taut against the weight all the time. The fibres will soon felt together, after which the twist will not unwind.

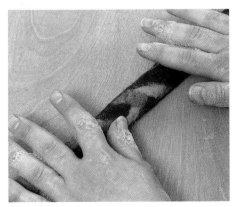

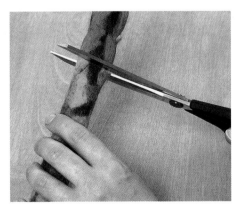

3 When the wool has felted on the outside, untie the string from the weight and roll the wool "sausage" firmly on the worktop to felt the fibres in the middle.

4 While the sausage is still flexible, cut off the ends tied with string. Wrap the felt around your wrist to check the fit and make sure that it will go over your hand when the ends are joined up. Trim down as required.

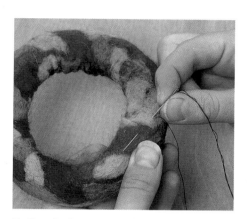

5 Stitch the two ends together using a long needle and strong thread. Take the thread from end to end inside the felt as well as stitching around the edges, to make the join very strong.

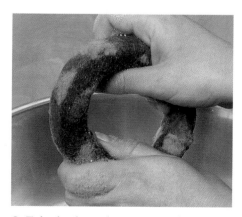

6 Felt the bracelet again in hot water and soap to shrink the inside curve and hide the stitches at the join. Rinse and allow to dry.

Felt brooches were popular in the 1930s and 1940s, when their bold colours gave a lift to a dull winter coat or plain hat. This design uses a thinner commercial felt than would have been available then.

Felt Flower Brooch

you will need

tracing paper, pencil, card (stock) and
scissors (for templates)

10 x 5cm/4 x 2in commercial
felt pieces, one each of pink,
mauve and orange

14.5 x 3cm/5¾ x 1¼in felt pieces,
one each of yellow and three
shades of green

scissors for cutting felt

needle and matching sewing thread

45cm/18in string

sewing machine

brooch back

1 Trace the templates from the back of the book. Transfer to the felt and cut out two flower shapes each in pink, mauve and orange, and four leaves in various shades of green.

2 Put the petals together in contrasting pairs. Now cut a fringed edge along three strips of yellow felt for the flower centres. Roll them up and place them in the centre of the paired petals.

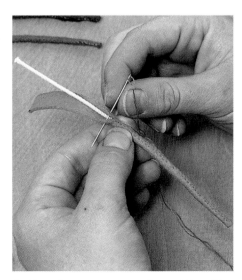

3 Stitch the flower centres in place. Pinch the backs of the petals, and stitch through all the layers to give the flowers more shape.

4 Cut the string into three 15cm/6in lengths, then slip-stitch a thin strip of green felt around each length to create the stalks.

5 Using a sewing machine, satin-stitch along the centre of each leaf to make a rib. Sew the four leaves together in a fan shape. Fold the stalks in half and sew them to the leaves. Then sew the flowers to the leaves over the folds of the stalks.

6 Now turn the brooch over and stitch the brooch back on very firmly, right in the centre.

A felt ball cut in half to reveal an intricate pattern makes a delightful pair of earrings. Cutting through the ball to reveal the marbled colours is so exciting it will probably prompt you to make more than one pair.

Marbled Earrings

you will need

5g/⅛oz fleece, in carded slivers, various colours

soap flakes

bowl

craft (utility) knife

felteen hat stiffener or PVA (white) glue

epoxy resin glue

earring posts and butterfly backs

1 Make a ball by twisting and wrapping two or more colours of fleece together. The more twists, turns and colours you use in the middle of the ball, the more intricate the resulting pattern will be. Dip the ball in hot, soapy water and squeeze and roll it to felt the fibres all the way through. When hard, rinse under a hot tap then a cold one.

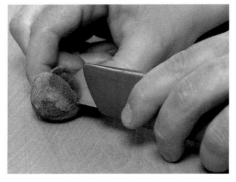

2 Leave the ball until it has dried out completely, then cut it in half using a craft knife. The pattern should stay in place; if the ball has not been felted all the way through, the middle will bulge out at this point.

3 To make the felt really hard, dip it in felteen hat stiffener. The felt must be absolutely dry as water reacts with the stiffener and will make a cloudy white film on the surface. An alternative is to dip the felt in PVA glue diluted with water, although this leaves a shiny surface.

4 Mix up a little two-part epoxy resin glue according to the manufacturer's instructions and use it to attach an earring back to the domed back of each earring.

These beaded felt buttons are ideal for a special cardigan or jacket, but they could also be used as eye-catching ornaments, or threaded on a leather thong, knotted at intervals, to make a necklace.

Acorn Buttons

1 Divide the brown and gold fleece into three and make each into three balls by dipping them in hot, soapy water and rolling in your hands. For the brown fleece, keep rolling and felting the balls until they are very hard and bounce when dropped.

2 For the gold fleece, squeeze and roll the balls as before but when they are beginning to go hard, distort them into the shape of rugby balls with your fingers. Rinse all the balls thoroughly in hot, then cold water.

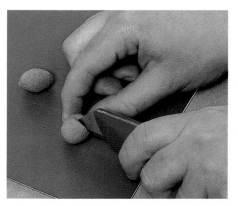

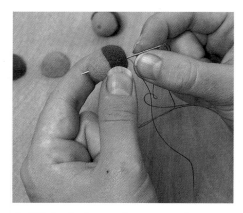

3 Leave the balls to dry out completely, then cut each one in half using a sharp craft knife. When halving the gold rugby balls, cut across the narrow width.

4 With their cut faces together, sew the gold half balls to the brown half balls using strong button thread. Make a stitch straight through the middle of each acorn and back, and pull the thread tight to form a small dimple at the top of each gold ball.

5 With the thread emerging from the base of the brown ball, make three small loops, one on top of the other, and use these as the foundation of a buttonhole shank.

6 Use polyester thread to sew beads round the rim of each acorn cup then spirally down to the shank to cover the cup. Sew the beads in groups of six: back-stitch three beads and catch down the thread before bringing the needle back out at the sixth bead.

Patterned ribbons can be irresistible and these tubular beads are an excellent way to make a feature of them. Mix and match the designs with coordinating small beads to make a necklace of subtle richness.

Ribbon Beads

you will need

white card (stock)

pencil

ruler

scissors

39cm/15in wire-edge patterned ribbon, 50mm/2in wide

PVA (white) glue

needle and matching sewing thread

round beads, 1.5cm/⅝in diameter

plastic-coated garden wire

75cm/30in toning ribbon, 3mm/⅛in wide

tubular beads

small gold beads

necklace clasp

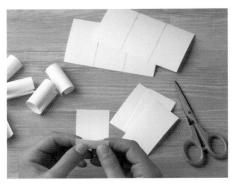

1 Cut six 7 x 4cm/2¾ x 1½in rectangles from the card and roll into tubes starting from one of the narrow ends.

2 Cut six 6.5cm/2½in strips of patterned ribbon, selecting the pattern area that you want to use along the ribbon. Now glue one end of each piece of ribbon on to the outside end of each tube of paper. Allow to dry completely.

3 Fold over the other end of the ribbon by 5mm/¼in. Roll the ribbon around the tube so that the edges of the ribbon meet. Stitch down the join. Push the wired edges of the ribbon into each end of the tube.

4 Apply glue to both ends of each covered tube and press a bead on to each end. Hold the beads in place while the glue dries by threading a piece of wire through each tube and bending the ends over.

5 Thread the ribbon-covered tubes on to the narrow ribbon, arranging round and tubular coloured beads and small gold beads in between them.

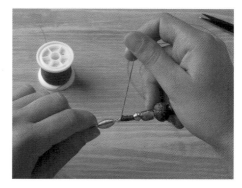

6 Thread a clasp on to the ends of the ribbon. Fold each ribbon end back on itself and stitch down, wrapping the thread over the stitching. Knot the end of the ribbon and wrap again with thread to cover the knot. Secure the thread firmly before cutting it off.

Romantic ribbon roses in harmonizing colours, framed by a circle of lace and trimmed with delicate streamers, create a charming posy effect for this hair ornament, which is ideal for a young bridesmaid.

Rose Hair Accessory

you will need

80cm/32in dark rose-pink ribbon, 2.5cm/1in wide

scissors

needle and matching sewing thread

40cm/16in warm beige ribbon, 2.5cm/1in wide

50cm/20in pale pink ribbon, 12mm/½in wide

30cm/12in cream ribbon, 10mm/³⁄₈in wide

60cm/24in dark rose-pink ribbon, 6mm/¼in wide

30cm/12in dark pink ribbon, 6mm/¼in wide

50cm/20in cream lace, 4cm/1½in wide

10cm/4in oval hairslide (barrette)

PVA (white) glue

20cm/8in each pale green, dark rose-pink and beige ribbon, 3mm/⅛in wide

1 Cut the 2.5cm/1in-wide dark rose-pink ribbon in half to make two large ribbon roses. Have a needle and thread ready for the final step. Fold the ribbon at a right angle, two-thirds along its length, and hold in place firmly.

2 Pass the long end under the triangular fold and hold with your other hand. Pass the short end under and hold, then continue to make concertina folds to the end of the ribbon.

3 Hold the two ends together, and gently grip with the thumb and forefinger of one hand. Carefully draw up the long end. This ruffles the ribbon and forms the rose petals.

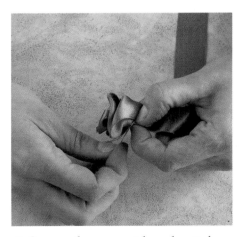

4 Secure the rose with stab stitches, being sure to pass through all the layers, then trim the ribbon ends. Make a second dark rose-pink rose, one warm beige, three pale pink, two cream, one small dark rose-pink and three dark pink roses in the same way.

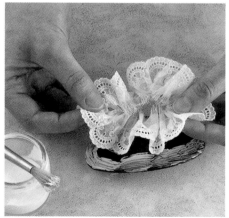

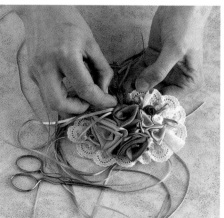

5 Gather the lace along its straight edge and draw it up in an oval shape to fit on to the hairslide. Tucking the raw ends neatly under, glue in place with PVA glue and leave to dry.

6 Arrange the ribbon roses inside the gathered lace and stick in place, one at a time, with the larger roses towards the centre framed by the smaller ones.

7 Cut several 4cm/1½in lengths of the green ribbon and stitch the ends together to form loops. Sew these between the roses around the outer edge. Make loops and streamers from the rest of the narrow ribbons and attach as shown.

Exuberant ribbon roses make a perfect hair accessory to go with a special party dress. Choose lavish satin and silk organza ribbons in shades that tone with your outfit and set off the colour of your hair.

Ribbon Rose Hairband

you will need

60cm/24in tartan ribbon,
6cm/2½in wide
needle and matching sewing thread
scissors
1m/1 yd each plain and gold-edged
green organza ribbons,
4 cm/1½in wide
satin-covered padded hairband
6 x 38cm/15in lengths of organza and
satin ribbons, 4cm/1½in wide

▲ **1** Make the central rose first. Fold one end of tartan ribbon at a right angle and twist it round twice, to form the centre. Secure at the bottom with a few stitches. Form the first petal by twisting the ribbon around the centre, folding it back at a right angle, so that the top edge lies across the "stalk", and catching it down with a secure stitch.

2 Continue to wrap the ribbon round in this way, securing each petal with a stitch. Finish off firmly, by stitching through all the layers.

▲ **3** Cut the green ribbon into 15cm/ 6in lengths and fold them to make leaves. Sew them to the centre of the hairband and then attach the rose in the middle.

4 Make six more roses in different colours and sew them along the hairband, interspersing them with more green leaves in both plain and gold-edged ribbon.

Join together vertical lengths of Fortuny-style pleated ribbon to make up a sculptural trinket bag. It's lined with iridescent fabric, and sparkling beads along the top edge add a pretty finishing touch.

Trinket Bag

you will need

1.6m/1⅝ yd pleated wire-edge ribbon, 50mm/2in wide

scissors

tape measure

dressmaker's pins

needle and matching sewing thread

40cm/16in pleated wire-edge ribbon, 56mm/2¼in wide

matching organza fabric

plate

pencil

sewing machine

38cm/15in fine matching cord

glass beads

1 To create the side of your trinket bag, cut the 50mm/2in-wide ribbon into eight pieces, with each piece measuring 20cm/8in in length. Now very neatly and firmly oversew the edges of these ribbon pieces together to form a tube.

2 For the bottom of the bag, simply stitch the two ends of the wider ribbon together.

3 Use a running stitch to gather one edge of the wider ribbon. Pull up the thread tightly and stitch to secure.

4 Slip-stitch the outer edge of the bottom of the bag to the lower edge of the side, turning in the raw edges.

5 For the lining, cut a rectangle 18 x 40cm/7 x 16in and a 14cm/5½in diameter circle from the organza. Use a suitable plate as a template.

▶

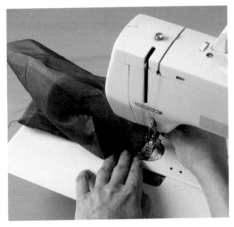

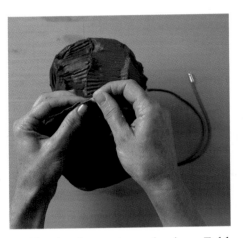

6 Machine-stitch the side seam, and pin and tack (baste) the side to the bottom of the bag. Machine-stitch together.

7 Fit the lining into the bag. Fold in the top edges of both the lining and the outer fabric and then slip-stitch the two together.

8 To make the carriers for the trinket bag's tie, cut two 6cm/2½in lengths of cord and poke the raw ends through a side seam on either side of the bag, 4cm/1½in from the top. Stitch securely in place. Now cut a piece of cord 25cm/10in long, fold it in half and knot the ends. Thread the loop through the tie carriers and pass the knotted ends through the loop.

Above: *Sumptuous pleated ribbons make an exquisite bag for small trinkets.*

9 As an attractive finishing touch, hand-stitch some decorative glass beads around the top edge of the bag at regular intervals.

This matching set is very easy to make in hooked ragwork. The domino spots, in loops of contrasting colour, stand out strongly against the cut pile background. Cotton jersey fabrics are ideal for this project.

Domino Hairslide and Earrings

you will need

pencil, ruler, card (stock) and scissors (for template)

30cm/12in square hessian (burlap)

felt-tipped pen

embroidery hoop

cotton jersey fabric in two contrasting colours

hook

scissors for cutting fabric

latex carpet adhesive

clear impact adhesive

10 x 4cm/4 x 1½in black felt (NB: extra will be needed for the earrings)

needle and matching sewing thread

hairclip fastening and earring clips

bonding adhesive

1 First, make yourself a card template that measures 10 x 4cm/4 x 1½in. Place it right in the middle of the piece of hessian and draw round it, using the felt-tipped pen. Now place the hessian piece in the embroidery hoop. Cut the jersey fabric into strips that measure 1cm/½in. Hook one of the colour blocks, making sure that you are working from the outside edge towards the centre.

2 Shear off the tops of the loops to create a cut pile surface. Repeat to make the second block of colour on the other half of the domino.

3 To make the spots for the domino, hook small loops in the contrasting colours. Do not cut these loops. Trim the excess fabric ends.

4 Remove the work from the hoop and place face down on a flat surface. Cut around the shape, leaving a border of 2cm/¾in all round. Apply a thin layer of latex adhesive over the back of the work and the border. Leave to dry for 5 minutes then turn in the border and press down firmly.

5 Apply clear impact adhesive to the back of the ragwork and cover with the black felt. Slip-stitch all round the edge. Attach the hairclip fastening to the back of the hairslide (barrette) using bonding adhesive and leave to dry for 1 hour. Make the earrings in the same way, using a 2.5cm/1in square template or a circle of the same size.

This set of hairslide (barrette) and hairbobbles is made from plastic carrier bags and remnants of nylon fabric! It shows what you can do at very little expense, and you can make the whole project very quickly.

Hooked Hair Accessories

you will need

pencil, ruler, card (stock) and scissors
(for template)

25cm/10in square hessian (burlap)

felt-tipped pen

embroidery hoop

nylon fabric

scissors for cutting fabric

coloured plastic carrier bags

hook

latex carpet adhesive

12 x 6cm/4¾ x 2½in black felt

needle and matching sewing thread

clear impact adhesive

hairclip fastening

bonding adhesive

elastic hairbands

1 Make a sawtooth card template measuring 11 x 5cm/4½ x 2in for the hairslide (barrette). Place it in the centre of the hessian and draw round it with a felt-tipped pen. Put the hessian in the embroidery hoop.

2 Cut the nylon fabric and the plastic into strips 1cm/½in wide. Start by hooking the fabric to outline the marked area, working in rows.

3 Using the plastic, hook loops to fill in the central triangles. Bring the ends of the fabric and plastic strips through to the top of the work as you reach them. Trim any excess lengths.

4 Remove the hessian from the embroidery hoop. Place face down on a flat surface and cut round the shape, leaving a border of 2.5cm/1in. Apply a thin layer of latex adhesive over the back of the work and the border. Leave to dry for 5 minutes, then turn in the edges and press down firmly.

5 Lay the card template on the black felt, draw round it and cut out the backing. Apply clear impact adhesive to the back of the ragwork. Place the felt on the back of the hairslide and slip-stitch in position.

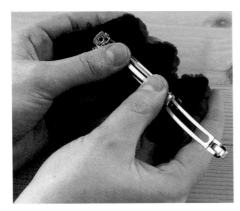

6 Carefully drop a small amount of bonding adhesive on to the top surface of the hairclip fastening, then hold it in position on the back of the hairslide. Leave to dry for 1 hour before wearing. Make the hairbobbles in the same way, using a round template of 2.5cm/1in diameter. Stitch the bobbles to the elastic hairbands.

This project uses a different ragwork technique to great effect. Fabric strips are wrapped round wire and bound with coloured embroidery threads, then coiled and sculpted into unusual brooches or earrings.

Wrapped Jewellery

you will need

three different fabrics

scissors

70cm/27½in wire

stranded embroidery thread (floss) in four colours, including a metallic thread

thick cotton thread

beads or sequins

pen or pencil

needle and matching sewing thread

brooch back

earring clips or wires

1 Cut the different fabrics into strips measuring 1cm/½in in width and the same length as the piece of wire. Starting at one end, wrap three different fabric strips round the wire, using embroidery thread to bind them in sporadic patches. When you are near the end of the wire, add a loop of thick cotton thread facing the end, and then continue wrapping the embroidery thread over this loop.

2 Thread the end of the embroidery thread into the loop with one hand, and with your other hand pull the two ends of the loop around until the thread end is tied off. Bind more embroidery thread in the other colours in patches along the length. Add a string of beads or sequins for extra decoration.

3 Wrap the metallic thread round one end, then wind it back on itself to tie in the end. Continue binding with the metallic thread, binding in the ends as before.

4 Wrap the finished bound length of wire around a pen or pencil to shape it into a spiral.

5 Remove the pen or pencil from inside the coiled length and sculpt it, working outwards and flattening it to make a cone shape. Stitch the fabric coils securely together and stitch on the brooch back. Make the earrings in the same way, but form the coiled lengths into lozenges instead of the cone shape. Stitch the earring findings to one end.

Even crisp (chip) packets can be hooked to make a loop pile surface just like fabric or yarn. In this heart-shaped brooch and matching ring the shiny plastic foil contrasts beautifully with the dark fabric border.

Crispy Brooch and Ring

you will need

pencil, card (stock) and
scissors (for template)
30cm/12in square hessian (burlap)
felt-tipped pen
embroidery hoop
scissors for cutting fabric
dark fabric
hook
foil crisp (chip) packets
latex carpet adhesive
12cm/5in square black felt
clear impact adhesive
needle and matching sewing thread
brooch back and ring fitting
bonding adhesive

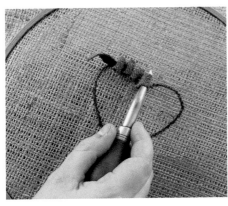

1 Make a cardboard template for your crispy brooch by drawing a heart shape that measures approximately 8cm/3in across. Now place the card template on to your hessian square and draw round it, using the felt-tipped pen. Place the hessian into the embroidery hoop.

2 Cut the dark fabric into strips 1cm/½in wide. Begin the hooking by following the outline of the heart shape. Make the loops close together, approximately 1cm/½in high.

3 Cut the crisp packets into strips 1cm/½in wide. Fill in the centre of the heart shape with loops of the same height as the fabric loops. Bring all the ends through to the top of the work, and trim any excess lengths.

4 Remove the hessian from the embroidery hoop and cut around the shape, leaving a border of 2.5cm/1in. Apply a thin layer of latex adhesive to the back and the border and leave to dry for 5 minutes.

5 Using scissors, make snips in the border at regular intervals. Turn in the border and press down firmly. Draw round the template on the black felt and cut out the backing. Apply clear impact adhesive to the back of the work, then cover with felt. Slip-stitch around the edge.

6 Position the fastening on the back of the brooch and stitch, using double thread. Make the ring in the same way, using a 2.5cm/1in diameter circle for the template. Attach the ring fitting with bonding adhesive.

Pompoms are easy to make, and can be threaded with beads to make this colourful, quirky necklace. These pompoms are made from cotton yarn with a rich velvety finish, but mixing yarns is also effective.

Pompom Necklace

you will need

pair of compasses

pencil

stiff card (stock)

scissors

darning needle

cotton yarn in various colours

60cm/24in round cord elastic

multicoloured wooden beads

1 With compasses, draw two 4cm/ 1½in circles on the card with 2cm/¾in circles within them. Cut round the outer and inner circles

to form two card rings. Thread the needle with yarn. Hold the two rings together with the end of the yarn under your thumb, and wrap the yarn around the rings.

2 When the rings are covered and the centre space filled, insert the scissors between the two card rings and cut around them, through all the loops.

3 Insert a length of yarn between the rings. Wrap it several times around the cut strands, tie in a knot and remove the rings. Trim the pompom neatly and make seven more, in different colours.

4 Thread the needle with elastic and start a repeated pattern of stringing three beads on to the needle and then pushing it through a pompom. Finish by knotting the elastic and threading the ends back through the beads.

Natural vegetable-tanned leather can be moulded with your fingers when dampened and is used here to decorate a hairband with flowers, which are easily coloured with permanent marker pens.

Floral Headband and Brooch

you will need

tracing paper, pencil, card (stock) and
scissors (for templates)

scraps of vegetable-tanned,
undyed leather

scissors for cutting leather

felt-tipped pens

sponge

PVA (white) glue

large brooch back

epoxy resin glue

elastic, 2cm/¾in wide

1 Following the templates at the back of the book, cut out all the elements for the headband and brooch from undyed leather. Using felt-tipped pens, colour in the leather "leaves" on the headband and brooch background. Using thin opaque pens, delineate outlines and markings on each flower. Then colour in with thicker translucent fluorescent pens.

2 Dampen all the elements with a moistened sponge, then shape the leaves and flowers with your fingers. Leave until completely dry. Scuff the surface of the leather on the headband and the brooch backing at the points of contact with the flowers. Then glue on the flowers with PVA glue. Attach the brooch backing with epoxy resin glue. Leave to dry.

3 Cut a V-shaped slot in each end of the headband backing. Cut the end of a piece of elastic into a point and slide it through one slot from front to back; glue into position with epoxy resin glue. Once dry, repeat with the other end, after trying on the headband to check the fitting.

The oak leaf motif is perfect for the warm autumnal colours of suede or leather. You'll need a tough piece of skin for the base layer of the hair ornament, but the buttons can be made from thin leather.

Oak-leaf Hair Clasp and Buttons

you will need

tracing paper, pencil, card (stock) and scissors (for templates)

pen

small, sharp scissors for cutting leather

small pieces of suede or leather in three colours

PVA (white) glue

stranded embroidery thread (floss)

sewing thread

small leather needle

glover's needle

pinking shears

hole punch

bamboo knitting needle

saw

abrasive paper

large self-cover buttons

1 Scale up the templates that have been provided for this project at the back of the book and then use them as guides to cut out two backing ovals and one front piece from different colours of either suede or leather. Now cut out your oak leaf stencil and then draw around it on to the top piece of suede.

2 Cut out the oak leaf shape from the suede using a pair of small scissors.

3 Glue the cut-out top piece on to the first backing piece using PVA glue. Leave to dry.

4 Stitch through the first backing piece with stranded embroidery thread to make a central leaf vein. Couch this down with sewing thread in a darker colour.

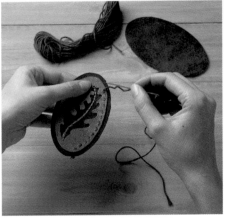

5 Using embroidery thread to match the backing leather and a glover's needle, make a running stitch border around the edge of the top piece.

6 Now neatly trim the edge of your first backing piece with the pinking shears. Then use more PVA to glue on the base layer. Once completely dry, use the pinking shears to trim the edge of this piece, too.

7 Carefully punch a hole at each side of the oak leaf using a No 6 hole punch. Saw a bamboo knitting needle down to a length approximately 5cm/2in longer than the hair clasp and rub the sawn end to a point with abrasive paper. Push the knitting needle down through one hole and out through the other.

8 Finally, to make the buttons, cut out circles of leather or suede large enough to cover the self-cover buttons. Cut out one oak leaf shape for each of the buttons from complementary colours of suede.

9 Glue each leaf to a backing circle. Lay a short length of stranded embroidery thread down the middle of the leaf and couch down with darker sewing thread.

10 Stretch the circle over the button dome, place the backing in position and snap it shut to secure.

Machine Embroidery

The versatility of machine embroidery enables needleworkers to experiment with a wide range of effects to produce truly original pieces. The great appeal of this craft is its speed – designs can be realized in a few hours and ideas captured with immediacy and spontaneity. Metallic threads are an ideal medium for this delicate form of jewellery: they can even be used on soluble material that is then dissolved to leave ethereal, glittering webs of stitches.

Most machine embroidery materials can be bought from craft suppliers. The most vital piece of equipment is, of course, a sewing machine, but it does not need a special embroidery programme.

Machine Embroidery Materials and Equipment

Darning foot

A darning foot is suitable for most embroidery, although fitting a presser foot gives a cleaner satin stitch. Alternatively, you can work without a foot, although the thread will tend to snap more frequently.

Embroidery hoops

A hand embroidery hoop can be used if the inner ring is wrapped in strips of cotton to hold the fabric taut. Special machine embroidery hoops with spring closures are more convenient.

Fabric

Calico provides a firm base for embroidery, but sumptuous fabrics such as shot organza, velvet and silk create a rich background. Felt can be used to back finished pieces.

Iron

Embroidery should be pressed on the wrong side to prevent scorching or flattening the stitches. Set a temperature that will not damage the least heat-tolerant part of the work.

Needles

Choose machine needles to match the thickness of the thread. Extra fine and metallic threads require 70/10 or 80/12 needles. For most other threads, 80/12 or 90/14 are suitable. Use a fine beading needle to attach tiny beads.

Non-woven interfacing

To stabilize fabrics for embroidery, back them with interfacing, which can later be torn away. Heavyweight interfacing can also be used alone as a base for filling stitchwork. Fusible interlining (interfacing) is used to bond layers of fabric together; templates can be drawn on the paper backing.

Sewing machine

The machine should have a free arm and a detachable bed for ease of movement. Make sure the feed can be lowered easily and that both top and bobbin tension can be adjusted. Clean and oil the machine regularly to keep it working smoothly.

Thread

Machine embroidery thread is available in different weights. Metallic threads come in shades of gold, bronze, silver and other colours, sometimes twisted with matt threads for a more subtle effect. Be careful when stitching metallics at high speed as they occasionally snap. Use invisible thread to stitch beads on to embroidery.

Water-soluble film

Using a stabilizer while stitching prevents puckering and distortion of openwork and sheer fabrics. As an alternative to non-woven interfacing you can use water-soluble film, which pulls away after immersion in cold water or can simply be torn away or dabbed with water to remove it. It can also be used to create pieces of free-standing embroidery.

If your sewing machine is capable of zigzag stitch you can use it to create many different effects: all the designs in this chapter are achieved by varying basic stitches. Start by practising simple shapes and outlines.

Machine Embroidery Techniques

Preparation

On a domestic sewing machine the direction and size of the stitch are controlled by the presser foot and the feed. If these are both removed stitches of any size can be made. Many machines have a darning function that lowers the feed; on others, the feed should be covered and the stitch length set to 0.

The fabric needs to be stretched taut on an embroidery hoop. Place it right side up in the outer ring and press the inner ring over it so that it lies flat on the machine bed.

Stitching

Practise stitching with the machine set at a slow speed if possible. Set the stitch width to 0 and lower the presser bar to engage the top tension. Work a few stitches to secure the threads then trim the ends to stop them tangling. You can either manoeuvre the hoop or place your fingers either side of the foot to guide the fabric. Keep it moving steadily and practise stitching in every direction, working spirals and filling stitches, drawing and writing.

For regular stitching the tension should be even top and bottom, but interesting effects can be achieved by altering it. If you loosen the bobbin tension, for example, the top thread

will lie on the surface as if couched. Different textures and weights of fabric will also have an effect on the stitching.

Stitch problems

Oil the machine regularly and remove lint and threads from the bobbin case. If stitches are not properly formed or the threads break, check first that the machine is correctly threaded, the needle is correctly fitted and is not blunt or bent, and that it is the appropriate size for the thread.

If the needle breaks

Check that the top tension is not too tight. If the fabric is moved too forcibly it can bend the needle, causing it to hit the needle plate or bobbin case.

If the top thread breaks

Check that the top tension is not too tight, the top thread is not knotted and the presser bar is lowered.

If the bobbin thread breaks

Check that the bobbin tension is not too tight, the bobbin thread is evenly wound, and there are no threads caught in the bobbin case.

If the fabric puckers

Check that the tension is not too tight, the stitches are not too long, and the thread is not too thick for the fabric (if it is, use a stabilizer under it). If the needle is hitting the bobbin case, the timing may be out and the machine will need servicing.

Transferring designs

Start by creating a template, scaling up the design if necessary using graph paper or the enlarge facility on a photocopier.

1 Transfer the design to a piece of thin card and cut it out. Lay the template on the fabric and draw around it with a water-soluble fabric pen.

2 If a design cannot be drawn on the fabric because of its texture, trace it on to a piece of water-soluble film and pin this to the right side of the fabric. Dissolve after stitching.

Stabilizers

Light fabrics may be distorted during embroidery if they are not stabilized with a firmer backing.

1 For heavy embroidery pin non-woven interfacing or lightweight paper to the wrong side of the fabric. It can be torn away after stitching.

2 Use water-soluble film to support lightweight fabric, lace or openwork during stitching.

Appliqué

Fabric shapes cut out using a template can be appliquéd to the base fabric using a plain zigzag stitch.

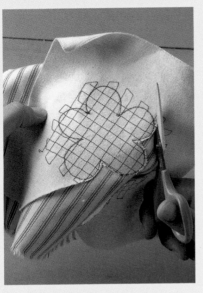

1 Draw the shape on the appliqué fabric, pin to the base fabric and stitch around the outline, then trim close to the stitching.

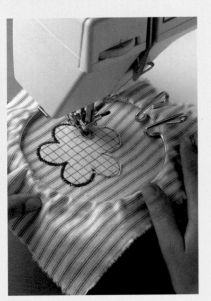

2 Or, draw the shape on fusible interlining (interfacing) and iron on to the base fabric. Cover the raw edge with zig-zag stitch.

Stitches   These stitches will all be useful when making jewellery and related items. Practise them on spare scraps of fabric, and experiment freely with different threads and tensions to create original effects.

Whip Stitch

Loosening the bobbin tension and tightening the top tension produces a beaded effect as the bobbin thread is brought to the surface. It is most effective when the bobbin is threaded with a contrasting colour.

Zigzag Filler

Set the stitch width as desired and move the fabric from side to side. To add shading, work several rows of stitching making the edges jagged so that subsequent layers will blend into the previous ones.

Looped Stitch

Work whip stitch, tightening the top tension and loosening the bobbin. Remove the top thread with a needle and bond a piece of fusible interlining to the wrong side to hold the looped stitches in place.

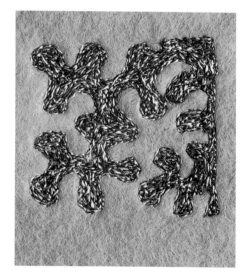

Couching

The fabric should be backed with a stabilizer. Lay a piece of thick thread or piping along the line of the design. Set the stitch width to the width of the piping and stitch down with a satin or zigzag stitch.

Satin Stitch

This can be worked in free embroidery or as regular stitching. Set the stitch width as desired; this can be varied along the line by altering the dial. Move the hoop slowly so that the stitches lie next to each other.

Double Threads

Thread two different threads through the needle together, using a large needle and a looser top tension to accommodate the extra thickness. This will give a subtle two-toned effect and tone down bright metallic threads.

Layers of contrasting fabrics and glittering machine embroidery make this a spectacular piece. The rough texture of the felts is wonderfully highlighted by shimmering organza and metallic machine embroidery.

Sparkling Starfish Brooch

you will need

pencil, thin card (stock) or paper and scissors (for templates)

dressmaker's pins

purple felt

tailor's chalk

fabric scissors

rust felt

shot organza

sewing machine with darning foot

needle size 70/10–80/12

metallic machine embroidery thread

needle and matching sewing thread

brooch back

1 Draw two freehand starfish shapes on to thin card or paper, one larger than the other. Cut the templates out roughly. Pin the large starfish template to the purple felt and draw around it with tailor's chalk.

2 Cut out irregular pointed shapes from the purple and the rust felt. Pin them down along the points of the starfish outline. Cut out the smaller starfish shape from organza and pin it on top of the felt starfish.

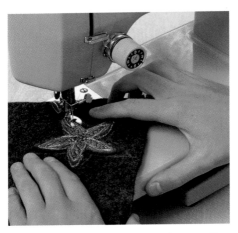

3 Thread the machine with metallic thread and stitch over the edges of the organza. Build up layers of texture and colour with different threads.

4 Cut out the felt starfish shape and a small circle of felt. Stitch this on to the centre back of the starfish. Stitch on the brooch back.

The heart is a timeless jewellery motif, evoking love and friendship. This filigree machine-embroidered hatpin, which can also be worn as a lapel pin, was inspired by baroque gilding found in a Czech church.

Heart Hatpin

you will need

water-soluble film

fabric pen

embroidery hoop

sewing machine with darning foot

needle size 70/10–80/12

metallic machine embroidery thread

thin jewellery wire

wire cutters

hatpin

beading needle

invisible thread

plastic beads in two sizes

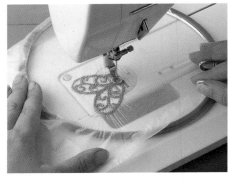

1 Copy the template from the back of the book, enlarging as required, and trace it on to water-soluble film with a fabric pen. Place the piece in an embroidery hoop and lower the sewing machine feed. Using metallic thread, stitch around the lines of the heart motif. Fill in the filigree outline, stitching in small circles.

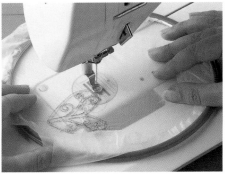

2 Stitch back and forth several times over the circular stitchwork. Remove the work from the machine and turn the embroidery the other way up in the hoop.

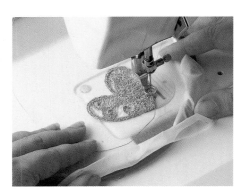

3 Set a narrow zigzag width. Curve a length of jewellery wire around the stitched outline of the heart, starting and finishing at the point at the bottom of the heart. Couch the wire in place and trim the ends.

4 Remove the piece from the hoop. Lay the hat pin in the centre of the heart. Set a medium zigzag width and couch the pin in place.

5 Immerse the piece in cold water and pull away the film. Using a beading needle and invisible thread, stitch the beads around the edge of the heart. Sew through a large bead, then a small one and back through the large bead. Make a stitch in the edge of the embroidery to secure the beads.

This exotic character with his flamboyant headdress is embroidered using filling stitchwork in richly contrasting threads on a background of interfacing, and is designed for stitching on to a blazer pocket.

Blazer Badge

you will need

pencil, thin card (stock) and scissors
(for template)

20cm/8in square non-woven
heavyweight interfacing

fabric pen

fabric paints

paintbrush

iron

sewing machine with darning foot

needle size 80/12–90/14

coloured and metallic machine
embroidery threads

needle and sewing thread

embroidery scissors

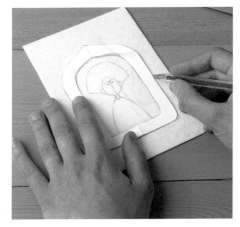

1 Follow the photograph opposite to draw the design, enlarging as required. Cut out a template from thin card. Lay this on a piece of interfacing and draw around the shapes with a fabric pen.

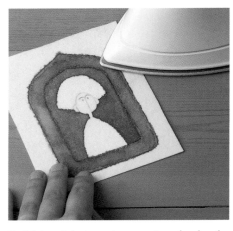

2 Using fabric paints, paint the background design in areas of solid colour, so that the white interfacing does not show through the stitching. Press with a medium-hot iron to fix the colours.

3 Lower the feed on the sewing machine. Fill in the design areas in the desired colours by working a straight stitch back and forth.

4 Work the face in a spiral from the centre point to the outline. To give a raised effect to the face, push the stitching out from the wrong side to form a dome shape.

5 Thread a needle with a dark thread and sew the eyes and nose details. Use gold thread to add the stars and the headdress details. Cut out the badge shape close to the outline. Set a medium stitch width and work a satin stitch all round the edge.

A decorative hatpin is a stylish way to jazz up a plain hat. This outsize brass pin is topped with an elaborate shining sun in machine-embroidered velvet, backed with rays of hammered metal.

Embroidered Sun Hatpin

you will need

yellow velvet

scissors

piece of any type of fine fabric

embroidery hoop

sewing machine with darning foot

needle size 80/12–90/14

coloured and metallic machine embroidery threads

brass sheet

tin snips

metal file

small ball hammer

brass wire

wire cutters

round-nosed (snub-nosed) pliers

epoxy resin glue

glass beads

hatpin

1 Cut out a yellow velvet sun. Place a piece of fine fabric in an embroidery hoop (to act as a stabilizer) and machine-stitch the sun to it. Thread the machine with contrasting threads in the top and bobbin and whip-stitch around the edge. Then make a deeper decorative band of stitching around the edge. Stitch a spiral on each ray in contrasting threads and finish with the face in the centre. Trim the velvet sun away from the fine fabric.

2 Cut out a larger sun shape from the brass sheet using tin snips, and file the edges until smooth. Hammer the brass to give it some interesting texture. To make an enclosure for the hatpin, form a spiral at each end of a piece of wire and hammer flat. Centre the wire over the brass sun and glue in place. Cut out a small circle of brass and glue over the wire.

3 Now glue the velvet sun on to the centre of the brass sun. Thread some glass beads on to the hatpin and glue them in place at the end. To assemble the finished piece, bend the wire spirals slightly backwards so that you can easily slide the hatpin through the top and bottom spirals.

A winged horse makes a stunning brooch, with subtle glints of light in the embroidery hinting at precious metal. The three-dimensional form is created after stitching and the back is varnished to hold the shape.

Horse Brooch

you will need

tracing paper, pencil, paper or card (stock)
and scissors (for templates)

20cm/8in square calico

scissors for cutting fabric

water-soluble film

dressmaker's pins

embroidery hoop

sewing machine with darning foot

needle size 90/14

metallic and coloured machine
embroidery threads

small piece of velvet

fine cord

acrylic varnish and paintbrush

beading needle

invisible thread

beads

brooch back

1 Copy the templates from the back of the book, enlarging as required. Cut the horse and wing shapes out of calico and pin them on to a piece of water-soluble film. Now place the piece in an embroidery hoop.

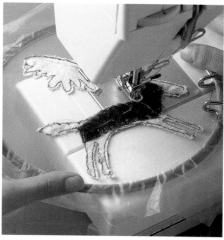

2 Lower the feed on your machine and stitch around the edges of the shapes. Cut some velvet to the shape of the horse's body and pin it in place. Fill the bobbin with contrasting thread and use two threads in the needle: one metallic and one coloured. Stitch over the velvet randomly to hold it in place.

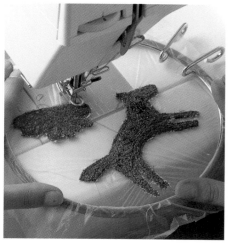

3 Fill in the wing area in a contrasting metallic thread. Stitch over the raw edges of each shape in small circles to neaten them.

4 Curve a length of fine cord around the outline of each shape. Set a medium zigzag width and couch the cord in place.

▶

5 Set the stitch width to 0. Work a narrow band inside the couched cord in a contrasting colour.

6 Take the embroidered pieces out of the hoop and immerse in cold water. Pull away the water-soluble film and leave to dry.

7 Stitch one end of the wing on to the horse's back using thread of a matching colour.

8 Shape the horse and the wing by curving them over your hand. To hold the shapes, paint two coats of acrylic varnish on to the wrong side of the pieces. Allow to dry.

9 Thread your beading needle with invisible thread and stitch small beads around the edges of the wing. Stitch a larger bead on to each hoof. Finally, stitch a brooch back on to the wrong side of the piece.

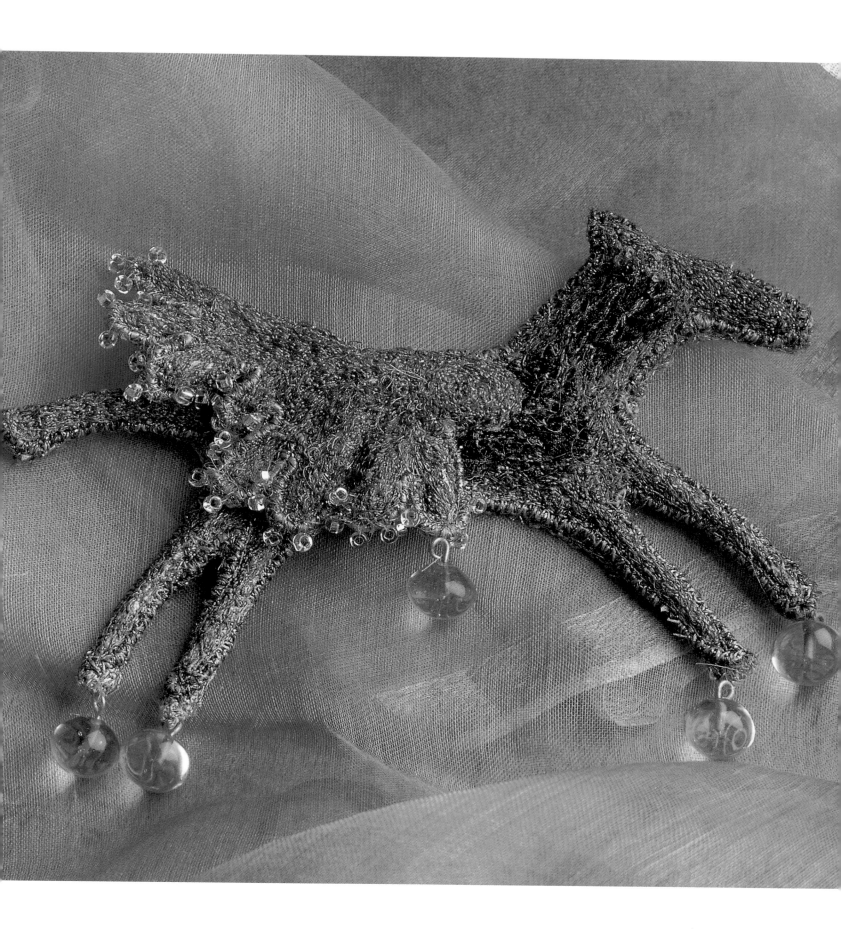

The intensely coloured ground fabric of this bracelet contrasts wonderfully with metallic embroidery in a strong, simple geometric pattern, embellished with embroidered domes topped with beads.

Harlequin Bracelet

you will need

pencil, ruler, paper or card (stock) and scissors (for template)

scissors for cutting fabric

30cm/12in square silk

fabric pen

iron

dressmaker's pins

non-woven interfacing

embroidery hoop

sewing machine with darning foot

needle size 80/90–12/14

metallic and coloured machine embroidery threads

embroidery scissors

metallic fabric paint

paintbrush

white paper

small coin

water-soluble film

beading needle

invisible thread

beads

brass jewellery wire

wire cutters

file

round-nosed (snub-nosed) pliers

clasp fastening

needle and matching sewing thread

1 First, cut out a paper or card template to the size required and then use this card template to cut out two pieces of silk, making sure that you leave a 2.5cm/1in seam allowance all around the edge. Now draw the pattern on to one of the pieces of silk with a fabric pen. Turn under the seam allowance on both pieces and press.

3 Working carefully, cut away the interfacing close to the machine stitching. Now paint diagonal lines between the stitched areas with your metallic fabric paint. Press the piece between two completely clean sheets of white paper, in order to fix the metallic paint.

2 Pin the patterned fabric to a piece of non-woven interfacing and place in an embroidery hoop. Lower the feed on the sewing machine. Fill the bobbin with contrasting thread and use a metallic thread in the needle. Using whip stitch, fill in each diamond and triangle shape, working in a spiral from the centre to the outside edge.

4 Use a coin to draw four circles on water-soluble film. With metallic thread on top and coloured thread in the bobbin, work back and forth from a circle's centre to its outline, then work a spiral from centre to outline. Immerse the piece in cold water, pull off the film and press each circle into a dome.

5 Thread a beading needle with invisible thread and sew a bead to the pinnacle of each dome. Stitch each dome at four points around its base over the point where two diamond shapes meet.

6 Cut seven pieces of jewellery wire 10cm/4in long. File the ends smooth and twist a spiral at each end using round-nosed pliers. Set a medium zigzag width and, using metallic thread, couch the wires on to the bracelet, one through each diamond and one at each end of the bracelet.

7 Pin the second piece of silk to the embroidered piece, wrong sides together. Set the stitch width to 0 and work a line of stitching all around the edge. Hand-stitch a clasp fastening to the ends of the bracelet.

These embroidered diamond-shaped earrings are padded to make them three-dimensional while remaining extremely light. A rich combination of colours and textures gives a precious, jewel-like quality.

"Diamond" Earrings

you will need

pencil, paper or thin card (stock) and scissors (for template)

fabric pen

small pieces of calico

small pieces of organza and silk

dressmaker's pins

sewing machine with darning foot

needle size 80/12

embroidery hoop

coloured and metallic machine embroidery threads

small, sharp scissors for cutting fabric

wadding (batting)

PVA (white) glue

2 small paintbrushes

metallic acrylic paint

needle

2 eye pins, 2 metallic beads and 2 glass beads

round-nosed (snub-nosed) pliers

earring wires

1 Cut out a diamond-shaped stiff paper or card template to the required size, and then use it to draw two diamond shapes on to the calico. Now draw four horizontal lines across each diamond, using a fabric pen. Pin a piece of organza over each marked shape. Lower the feed on the sewing machine and place the fabric in an embroidery hoop. With matching thread, stitch the horizontal lines and several lines around the design.

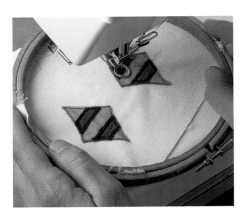

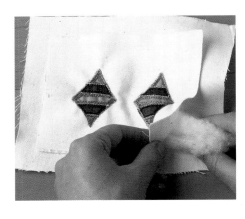

◀ **4** Pin a second piece of calico to the wrong side of the embroidery. Place it in the hoop and stitch around three sides of each diamond. Stuff both diamonds with wadding, right into the corners. Close up the fourth side with stitching. Cut out the shapes close to the stitched outline. With a brush, apply PVA glue to the edges of the shapes to varnish and stiffen them. Leave to dry.

▲ **2** Now, working very carefully, use your scissors to trim away the excess organza, cutting close to your stitched outline.

◀ **3** Cut two pieces of silk in a contrasting colour. Pin them over the diamonds. Place the piece in a hoop. Stitch some lines around the horizontal stripes with matching thread. Trim off excess fabric close to these lines. Work lines of stitching around the stripes to cover raw edges, plus more lines around the design with metallic thread.

5 Now paint the back and the edges of the diamond shapes, using metallic acrylic paint. When the paint has dried, make a hole at the top of each diamond with a needle. Thread each eye pin through a small metallic bead, a glass bead and then the embroidered diamond. Using round-nosed pliers, twist the wire at the back to secure in place and attach the earring wires to the eye pins.

This unusual fan-shaped comb is decorated with deeply worked embroidery. There are no solid areas of colour, but a subtle, densely mottled surface created by whip stitching one colour over another.

Glittering Hair Comb

you will need

tracing paper, pencil, paper or thin card (stock) and scissors (for templates)

fabric pen

18cm/7in square calico

scissors for cutting fabric

water-soluble film

dressmaker's pins

embroidery hoop

sewing machine with darning foot

needle size 80/12

coloured and thick metallic machine embroidery threads

brass jewellery wire

wire cutters

hair comb

needle and matching sewing thread

self-adhesive felt

1 Copy the templates from the back of the book, enlarging as required, and draw around them on to the calico. Now cut out the fabric pieces and pin them to water-soluble film. Place the whole piece in an embroidery hoop. Lower the feed on the sewing machine. Using contrasting threads in the bobbin and the needle, work whip stitch in circles to fill in the outline. Stitch areas of different colours bleeding into each other to give a mottled effect. Stitch in circles to neaten the raw edges.

2 Turn the piece over in the hoop. Fill the bobbin with metallic thread and use contrasting thread in the needle. Work a whip stitch along the zigzag edge of the larger piece.

◄ **3** Immerse the pieces in cold water and pull away the film. Cut a 2.5cm/1in square of card and eight 1m/1 yd lengths of jewellery wire. Wrap a length of wire around the card. Cut the wire at one end and twist the strands together at the other end to make a tassel. Repeat with the other lengths. Set a medium zigzag width and, using metallic thread, couch the tassels in place between the points on the larger piece of embroidery.

4 Lay the smaller piece on top of the larger, matching up the lower edges. Set the stitch width to 0 and join the two pieces using matching thread, stitching in circles. Hand-stitch the top bar of the hair comb to the lower edge of the embroidered piece. Draw around the larger template on to a piece of self-adhesive felt and cut out the shape. Peel off the paper backing and stick the felt on to the back of the embroidery.

This stunning necklace features cords that appear to be wrapped but are in fact embroidered. Unusually shaped beads picking up a colour in the stitchwork are suspended between the cords on jewellery wire.

Beaded Necklace

you will need

sewing machine with darning foot

needle size 90/14

fine metallic and coloured machine embroidery threads

40cm/16in and 72cm/29in lengths thick cord

60cm/24in thin cord

pencil, stiff paper or thin card (stock) and scissors (for template)

pen

felt

scissors for cutting fabric

dressmaker's pins

water-soluble film

embroidery hoop

pin board

needle and matching sewing thread

round-nosed (snub-nosed) pliers

brass jewellery wire

wire cutters

beads

necklace clasp

1 Lower the feed on the sewing machine. Fill the bobbin with a metallic thread and use a coloured thread in the needle. Set a medium to wide zigzag width and feed each of the cords through the machine several times, changing the colours each time to give a mottled effect. Create bobbles at intervals along the cords by stitching back and forth over a point with metallic thread.

2 Draw a heart shape approximately 1cm/½in tall on thin card. Use this template to draw four hearts on a piece of felt and cut them out. Pin the felt hearts on to a piece of water-soluble film and place in an embroidery hoop. Set the stitch width to 0 and fill in the shapes with whip stitch, spiralling outwards from the centre to the edge. Immerse the piece in water and pull away the film.

3 On a pin board, pin out the shortest length of cord to make the inner ring and the medium length 2cm/¾in from the first to make the outer ring. Pin the longest length of cord around the outer ring, making curves along its length. Hand-stitch the points where the curves meet the outer ring. Using pliers, bind the ends of the cords

together with brass jewellery wire. Cut 22 pieces of wire, each 5cm/2in long, and thread a bead on to each one. Using pliers, twist one end of each wire around the inner cord and the other end around the outer cord. Attach some of the beaded wires between the curved cord and the outer ring. Trim the ends of the wires.

4 Cut four 6cm/2½in lengths of wire. Use a needle to pierce a hole at the top and bottom of each embroidered heart. Thread each wire through a bead, then through the heart and through another bead. Twist the ends of each wire into spirals and attach both ends to the cords. Hand-stitch the clasp to the ends of the cords.

Metallic threads, iridescent paper and shimmering beads combine to make these glittering pieces of jewellery. The embroidery is done on a base that dissolves to leave only the sparkling tracery of stitches.

Iridescent Earrings and Pendant

you will need

water-soluble film

embroidery hoop

dressmaker's pins

tracing paper, pencil, stiff paper or thin card (stock) and scissors (for templates)

fabric pen

iridescent paper

sewing machine with darning foot

needle size 90/14

metallic machine embroidery threads

general-purpose scissors

iron

kitchen paper

self-hardening clay

stiff wire

blue-green watercolour inks

paintbrush

metallic paints

card

felt

plastic sheet

acrylic spray varnish

beading needle

selection of small beads

2 split rings

pliers

2 jump rings

earring wires or posts

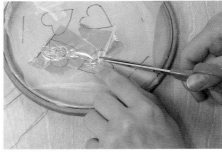

1 Stretch a layer of water-soluble film in an embroidery hoop and then pin another layer to the back. Copy the templates provided at the back of the book, enlarging them if necessary, and draw round them on the film. Now pin pieces of iridescent paper to the back of the film over the centres of the motifs. Thread the bobbin and needle with metallic thread. Set the machine stitch width to 0 and lower the feed. Work stitching in circles around the centres of the motifs and then carefully cut away any excess iridescent paper from the back.

4 Make small balls of self-hardening clay for the beads, and push them on to a stiff wire. Leave to dry, stuck into a piece of clay.

2 Machine-stitch right around the outlines of the motifs, and then fill in the area around the centres with whip stitch, spiralling outwards to the edge.

3 Immerse the embroidery in water to dissolve the film. Iron dry between kitchen paper.

5 Paint the clay beads with blue-green watercolour inks. Leave to dry, then add highlights with dots of metallic paint.

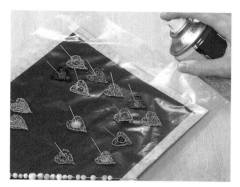

6 Cover a large piece of card with felt and then with plastic sheet, to make a soft backing sheet. Pin the motifs to the backing and coat the clay beads and the embroidered motifs with acrylic spray varnish.

7 Using a beading needle, attach metallic thread to the top of a motif. Thread on two small beads, then a clay bead and two more small beads. Take the thread through a split ring and then back down again through the beads and into the motif. Fasten off. Sew a ring of small beads around the centre of the motif.

8 To make an earring, open a jump ring with pliers and thread through the split ring. Join it to the ring on the earring wire or post. If you are making a pendant, then thread a machine-embroidered chain through the slip ring.

Beads and Shells

Strings of beads are perhaps the simplest, most primitive form of personal adornment, but they are infinitely adaptable, and new ways of decorating with beads are constantly being devised. Modern beads are available in an enormous range of materials, shapes and textures, from glass and metal to semi-precious stones. Shells, which are beautiful natural objects in their own right, are equally versatile starting points for inspirational jewellery designs.

Many craft suppliers specialize in beads, and finding a particularly beautiful example is often the inspiration for a piece of jewellery. Only a few other basic materials are needed for most projects.

Beadwork Materials and Equipment

Bead loom

This small loom is specially designed for use with beading thread, and enables you to weave narrow bands of small beads in colourful patterns. They can be turned into items such as bracelets and headbands. The warp threads are wound around wooden rollers at each end of the loom and fitted between metal springs to space them evenly.

Beading needles

Fine, long beading needles can be used to thread several beads at a time, so are particularly useful when working with tiny beads. They need careful handling as they break easily.

Beading thread

Fine, strong nylon thread is specially designed for beadwork, though a strong smooth thread such as polyester may be equally effective. Large beads can also be threaded on decorative yarns such as silk.

Beading wire

Gold, copper and silver wire are available in many gauges: 0.4mm (gauge 30 or 25) and 0.6mm (gauge 22) are the most useful. Check that the wire will fit through the holes in the beads.

Beads

Glass – Glass beads are available in every colour and size, from tiny seed beads and rocailles to large, decorated Venetian and drop beads. Small beads are sometimes sold pre-strung: this makes them easy to transfer to a beading needle, but they are also ideal for stitching down in couched designs.

Indian lampwork beads sometimes have an insert of foil and are decorated with molten glass patterns. To make wound beads, molten glass is wound around a rotating metal rod to create swirling striped patterns.

Metal – These beads often have sophisticated shapes and are made in copper, brass and other alloys; they may also be plated with gold or silver. Small metal spacer beads are often used to separate larger beads or at the end of a string.

Natural materials – Mother-of-pearl, bone and wooden beads are all available in many shapes and sizes.

Beeswax

Waxing beading thread strengthens it and helps to prevent it snagging on sharp edges, which is especially useful when threading faceted beads.

Cord

Threaded small beads can be wrapped around a core of three-ply piping or furnishing cord to make chunky pieces of jewellery.

Cotton spheres

These and other shapes made of compressed cotton fibres are available from beading suppliers.

Self-cover buttons

Sold in kit form in a range of sizes, these can be covered with fabric on to which beads can be stitched.

Fabric paint

If fabric is used as a foundation for beadwork, it may need to be coloured to match the beads. For small projects a permanent fabric pen can be used.

Glue

Epoxy resin glue or a glue gun can be used to attach small beads.

Palettes

Decant beads into white china artist's palettes or saucers to keep colours separate and make them easier to pick up.

Round-nosed (snub-nosed) pliers

Jewellery pliers are essential for shaping wire in small coils and for opening and closing rings and other findings.

Scissors

An old pair of scissors can be used to crack damaged or misplaced beads so that they can be removed from a string without unthreading all the others.

Tweezers

These are useful for both selecting and removing very small beads.

Shells are found in an amazing variety of shape, size, colour and texture, making them a fascinating craft medium. Stylish modern jewellery designs are an ideal setting for their natural, subtle beauty.

Shellwork Materials and Equipment

Assorted shells

Beautiful shells have been keenly collected for centuries, and their desirability has inevitably led to their exploitation in trade. Taking attractive and sometimes rare shells from their natural habitat – perhaps with their original owners still inside them – can result in the depletion of marine species. Consequently, shell-

collection and export has now been made illegal in some parts of the world. It's important to make sure that any shells you use have been gathered in a responsible way.

Beachcombing is an enjoyable activity when you are at the seaside, and huge drifts of small shells can sometimes be found washed up along the beach. In these circumstances a

small number can safely be collected as long as you make sure they are empty when you pick them up.

Other environmentally sound sources of shells include fish dealers and restaurants and old shell necklaces and other craft items. If you eat shellfish such as cockles and mussels at home you can simply save the shells; otherwise they are regularly discarded

by restaurant kitchens and if you make friends with your local seafood restaurant the staff may be happy to save some for you.

Old shell necklaces and trinkets are a very good source of small shells for jewellery-making, with the advantage that the shells are already drilled for threading. They're cheap and easy to find at flea markets and jumble sales.

Dust mask

Always wear a mask when sanding shells to avoid inhaling the dust.

Glue

A glue gun is useful for attaching shells quickly and accurately, but epoxy resin glue or PVA (white) glue are also suitable. Epoxy putty comes in two parts that are mixed together just before use. It is a strong adhesive that can be used to fill small shells to take button backs and other fittings.

Goggles

Wear protective goggles when drilling or sanding shells.

File

Use a small file to smooth any rough edges on shells that might catch on skin or clothing.

Ink

To colour shells, inks containing shellac are ideal. They can be mixed or watered down to achieve subtle shades and are waterproof once dry.

Mini-drill

A small electic drill is the most useful tool you can invest in for any kind of shellcraft. The very small bits will enable you to drill tiny holes in the most fragile of shells. Other attachments are available for smoothing surfaces, grinding rough edges and polishing shells until they shimmer.

Reusable putty adhesive

Press shells into a blob of putty on the work surface to hold them securely while you are drilling them.

Ribbons

Choose ribbons with a seaside feel – such as checks and stripes in fresh colours – for shellcraft projects, or use delicate pinks and creams to match the colours of the shells.

Stone-effect beads

Natural-looking beads in a variety of shapes combine well with shells.

Tweezers

A pair of tweezers may be helpful for picking up and positioning tiny shells.

When threading beads or shells, it's important that the thread you choose is strong enough to support their weight. Shells need to be drilled for threading, and may be polished to enhance their natural beauty.

Bead and Shellwork Techniques

Pre-strung Beads

Small glass beads are often supplied pre-strung, making them ideal for creating pieces such as rope necklaces or for attractive couched designs.

1 In order to re-thread pre-strung beads, thread a beading needle and pass it through the beads. Once you have the length that you need, then simply remove the old thread from the string.

2 For a couched design, lay a length of pre-strung beads down on a piece of fabric following the line of a design. Now stitch over them, positioning your stitches between the beads, to secure.

Threading a Bead Loom

Bead weaving produces narrow, flat strips of beaded fabric. The beads lie between the warp threads, and a continuous weft thread is passed through the beads, weaving over and under the warp threads.

1 Cut the warp threads to the length of the finished piece plus 45cm/18in. Cut one thread for each bead across the width, plus one extra. Lay the threads out smoothly and knot them at each end. Divide the strands in half and slip one knot over the rivet in the roller. Wind on the threads then arrange them evenly in the spring.

2 Slip the knot at the other end of the warp threads over the rivet in the other roller and wind on as before until the warp threads are taut.

3 Thread a beading needle with a long length of thread and draw it through beeswax. Tie the end of the thread to the first warp thread 2.5cm/1in from the roller.

Needle-woven Beading

In this beading technique, a continuous thread is taken through successive rows of beads, with the second row fitting between pairs of beads in the first. The second row is joined to the first by interweaving. For a long piece such as a necklace that does not need a clasp, the work can be done in rounds; for shorter pieces work the second row in the opposite direction to the first. Additional rows can be added in the same way, woven into the preceding row of beads.

1 Thread on the required number of beads for the first row. Knot the ends of the thread if working in rounds.

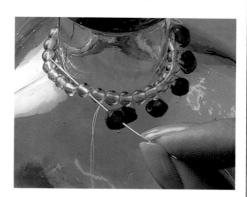

2 Pass the needle through the first bead of row 1, then through the first bead of row 2, then the third bead of row 1. Repeat to the end of the row.

Sanding and Polishing Shells

1 Using a coarse sanding disc on a mini-drill, remove the outer coating of the shell and smooth down the ridges.

3 Use a woolly mop head to shine the inner surface of the shell.

Amazing results can be achieved by sanding and polishing ordinary shells such as these green mussels. Always wear a dust mask and goggles.

2 Switch to a fine sanding disc to strip the shell down to mother-of-pearl (the shell will now be very fragile).

4 To get into the corners, use a conical felt mop.

Drilling Shells

A mini-drill can be used to make holes in small shells. The more fragile the shell, the finer the bit should be and the slower the drilling speed.

Before you start drilling, secure each shell to the work surface with reusable putty and hold it firmly in place as you work. Judging the right place to make a hole is often a matter of instinct.

These delicate gold wire earrings take the form of tiny sets of scales filled with beads in shades of green and blue. Thread the same number of beads into each basket so that the scales balance.

Beaded Balance Earrings

you will need

fine brass beading wire

fine crochet hook

round-ended pencil

selection of small glass beads

round-nosed (snub-nosed) pliers

4 jump rings

2 split rings

earring posts with loops and butterfly backs

20 gauge/0.8mm/0.03in brass wire

wire cutters

1 Using the fine brass beading wire, crochet four round shapes that measure 1cm/½in across. On the last round make three 2cm/¾in equally spaced loops. Leave a long end of wire. Twist the loops.

2 Mould each round into a dome shape over the end of a pencil. Thread equal numbers of beads on to the loose end of wire and secure them in each basket. Do not trim the wire yet.

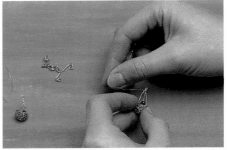

3 Using pliers, attach a jump ring, then a split ring, to each earring fitting. Cut two 4cm/1½in lengths of the 20 gauge wire. Twist an upward loop in the centre of each, then bend the ends down into two loops from which the baskets will hang. Attach the centre loop to the split ring using another jump ring. Thread the long end of wire on one basket through the top of the twisted loops to bring them together and attach to the bar. Repeat with the other baskets. Trim the ends of the wire.

Ornate hatpins were once an indispensable fashion accessory, as no lady would venture out without a hat. These contemporary versions could be worn on a lapel if you don't need them to hold a hat in place.

Ornate Beaded Hatpins

you will need

decorative and diamanté beads

hatpin bases with safety ends

glue gun or clear impact adhesive

lengths of ribbon in several colours,
6mm/¼in wide

needle and matching sewing thread

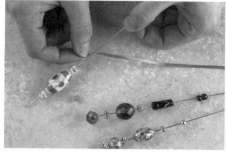

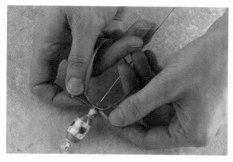

1 Choose a selection of beads in matching or complementary colours and in various shapes and sizes. Pick out a small bead to put on the pin first to prevent the others slipping off the end. Smear the shaft of the pin with a very thin coat of glue, then add the other beads.

2 Streamers can be added by threading a length of narrow ribbon between the beads. Tie into a bow and secure with a few stitches.

3 To create a flowered effect, twist lengths of narrow ribbon into a few tiny roses. Sew a few stitches through the base of each flower to secure, then glue the roses between the beads.

In this sumptuous creation, multiple strands of beads are joined at intervals with large Venetian beads – this is an ideal way to show off a few precious beads by mixing them with small beads in toning colours.

Venetian Necklace

you will need
beading needle
scissors
strong black nylon thread
5mm/³⁄₁₆in lilac iridescent and red glass beads
3mm/¹⁄₈in bronze and green glass beads
7 large Venetian glass beads
2 crimping beads with loops
round-nosed (snub-nosed) pliers
2 x 5mm/³⁄₁₆in gold loops
S-shaped gold fastener

1 Thread a needle with 250cm/100in of nylon thread and knot the ends together. Tie a bead to the end, as an anchor. Thread beads on the double thread as follows (just a suggestion, those seen opposite are different): one lilac, 25 bronze, one green, two bronze, two green, one red, three green, one red, one lilac, one Venetian, one lilac, one red, three green, one red, two green, two bronze, one green. Repeat the sequence six more times. End with 25 bronze beads and a lilac one.

2 Cut another 250cm/100in length of thread, thread through the needle, knot and tie around the anchor bead as before. Pass the needle through the first lilac bead threaded in step 1 then thread on 25 bronze, one green, two bronze, two green, one red and three green. Pass the needle through the red, lilac, Venetian, lilac and red beads threaded in step 1. Repeat this sequence six more times, ending with 25 bronze beads and passing the needle through the last lilac bead.

3 Make another three interwoven strands in the same way. Tie the threads in a tight knot at each end, then attach a brass crimping bead over each knot and close with pliers.

4 Attach a gold loop to the top of each crimping bead. Thread the fastener through the loops.

Small plastic boxes with well-fitting lids can be used to keep all kinds of small treasures safe. Recycle one with style, jazzing it up with glass paints in strong colours and a sprinkling of tiny, glittering seed beads.

Glittering Trinket Box

you will need

clear plastic box

black relief outliner

ruler

flat-backed gold bead

all-purpose glue

small glass beads

glass paints in dark brown, crimson and yellow

medium and fine paintbrushes

kitchen paper

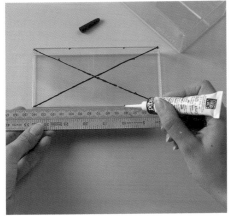

1 Mark out a simple geometric pattern on the lid of your box, using black relief outliner. Use a ruler to make sure that you keep all of your lines straight.

2 Rest the outliner on the ruler to guide it when you are outlining the edge of the lid.

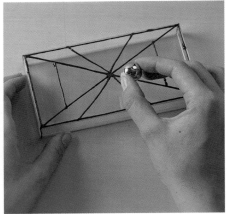

3 While the outliner is still wet, press a flat-backed gold bead into the centre. As it dries, the outliner will hold the bead securely in place.

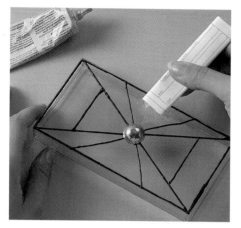

4 Cover the four panels on the cross on the lid with a thin layer of all-purpose glue.

5 While the glue is wet, sprinkle small glass beads on to the surface and let them stick.

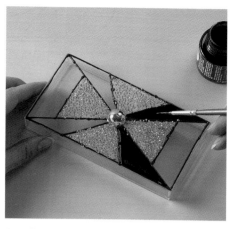

6 Fill in the areas between the beaded panels on the lid using the dark brown glass paint.

7 Paint the remaining areas on top of the lid in crimson.

8 Paint the sides of the lid in crimson, and leave to dry.

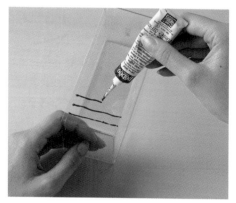

9 Using black outliner, draw vertical lines down the sides of the box at 1cm/½in intervals.

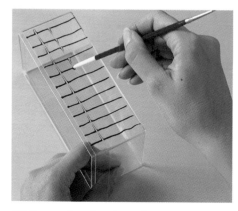

10 Immediately, drag the pointed end of a paintbrush through the lines to break them up. Drag the brush in alternate directions at 1cm/½in intervals down the sides, wiping the excess paint off the brush at the end of each stroke. Leave for at least an hour to dry.

11 Use a fine paintbrush to paint alternate stripes in crimson along the sides of the box.

12 Paint the remaining stripes around the sides in bright yellow and leave to dry completely.

Cord beading, in which strings of small beads are wound around and then stitched on to a readymade cord core, is very popular with the Zulu people, who are among the world's most skilled beadworkers.

Cord-beaded Bracelet

1 Bind both ends of the cord tightly with thread to stop them unravelling. Paint the cord with fabric paint in a colour that matches the beads, so that it will not show through.

2 Thread the needle and make a few stitches at one end of the cord. Thread on 20 beads, holding the thread taut and pushing the beads together. Wind the beads around the cord, make a couple of stitches then pass the needle back through the last few beads. Repeat along the length of the cord.

3 To finish the ends of the cord, thread on a few beads and make a stitch across the blunt end. Make several more stitches to completely cover the end.

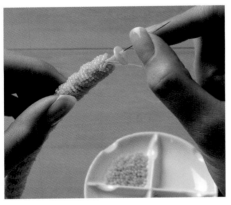

4 Make a beaded loop at one end of the cord large enough to fit the button. At the other end, thread on three beads then pass the needle through the button. Thread on two more beads, pass the needle back through the button and make several stitches to finish off.

This pretty scalloped tiara is heavily encrusted with spirals of artificial pearls. The backing is stiffened with wire and stitched to a hair comb, and the tiara would be ideal to hold a bridal veil in place.

Pearl Tiara

you will need

tracing paper, pencil, card (stock) and scissors (for template)

non-woven heavyweight interfacing

fabric pen

scissors for cutting fabric

17.5cm/7in millinery wire

round-nosed (snub-nosed) pliers

needle and matching

sewing thread

beading needle

beading thread

1cm/½in pearl bead

6mm/¼in pearl beads

4mm/⅕in pearl beads

4 x 8mm/⅖in pearl beads

4 drop pearl beads

plastic hair comb

1 Copy the template from the back of the book on to card, scaling up as necessary, and cut out. Place your card template on to the interfacing, draw around it twice, and cut out. Bend a loop at each end of the millinery wire. Now stitch the wire to one piece of the interfacing 2cm/¾in from the straight edge.

2 Following the template guide, mark the centre of each scallop on the right side of the wired interfacing. Stitch the 1cm/½in pearl bead to the centre of the middle scallop. Bring the needle through to the right side next to it and thread on eight 6mm/¼in beads and enough 4mm/⅕in beads, spiralling outwards, to fill the scallop shape, then make a fastening stitch to secure.

3 Thread a sewing needle with matching thread and make tiny stitches over the beading thread in between the pearl beads. Repeat for the other scallops, using 8mm/⅖in beads in the centre of each. Couch down the small beads to fill in all the remaining areas of interfacing.

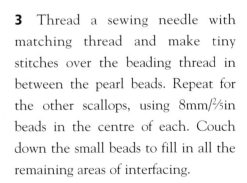

4 Slip-stitch the back piece of the tiara to the front. Stitch the drop beads between the scallops.

5 Stitch the comb to the back of the tiara, catching it along the bottom edge of the beaded piece.

The starting point for this necklace was the unusual filigree pendant at the centre. The beads are strung on a length of knotted silk, created by working blanket stitch around a core of thread.

Chinese Necklace

you will need

2-ply silk thread

scissors

tape measure

drawing pins (thumb tacks)

pinboard

fine silk thread

2 large-eyed needles

6 bone beads

2 round amber beads

2 round lampwork beads with foil inserts

4 precious stone beads

3 lampwork discs with foil inserts

2 large amber beads

large Chinese pendant

necklace clasp

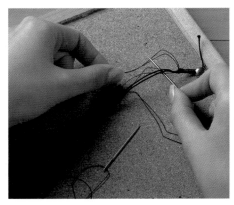

1 For each side of your Chinese necklace, cut a 1m/1 yd length of 2-ply silk thread. Fold in half and pin the midpoint to a pinboard. Cut two 2m/2 yd lengths of fine silk. Thread each on to a large-eyed needle, double the thread, tie a knot and slip both knots over the pin. Lay the fine silk thread next to the 2-ply lengths. Work a blanket stitch along the threads for 12cm/4½in.

2 Now carefully separate the 2-ply silk strands and, using the two needles and the fine silk, work a blanket stitch for 2.5cm/1in down each strand individually.

3 Thread a bone bead on to one strand and a round amber bead on to the other. Tie double knots just beneath the beads. Continue as for step 1 for another 1.5cm/⅝in.

4 Thread on a round lampwork bead and tie a knot just beneath it. Continue as one strand for 1.5cm/⅝in, divide in two for 1.5cm/⅝in, thread on two precious stone beads, tie knots.

5 Continue as two strands for 1.5cm/⅝in, join and continue as one strand for 1cm/½in, thread on a lampwork disc, knot, continue as one strand for 1cm/½in. Thread on a bone, a large amber and another bone bead, knot, and continue as one strand for 1cm/½in. Make the other side of the necklace to match. Tie the two sides together, thread all ends through the large pendant and knot.

6 Thread the ends through a lampwork disc and knot. Thread the ends back through the disc and trim. Remove the piece from the board and stitch the necklace clasp to each end.

Satisfying to make, any of these lovely buttons would add a unique touch to a special garment. The luscious blackberry would look equally attractive as a pendant hanging from a bracelet or necklace.

Beaded Buttons

1 For the blackberry button, use a black felt-tipped pen to cover the cotton sphere completely. Thread a needle with black sewing thread and make a few stitches at the top of the sphere to secure the end.

2 Thread on a small black glass bead, make a stitch then pass the needle right through the sphere. Thread on another bead and stitch down. Take the needle around the sphere, passing through the two beads at top and bottom, then around at right angles to divide it into quarters.

3 Thread on 18 beads and pass the needle through the bead at the bottom of the sphere. Thread on 18 more beads and pass the needle through the top bead. Repeat, taking more beads around the sphere at right angles.

4 Thread on 16 beads and work from top to bottom as before, this time dividing the sphere into eight sections. Repeat with 14 beads, dividing the sphere into 16 sections, until the whole sphere is covered.

5 If the blackberry is intended to hang on a bracelet or necklace, secure a thread at the bottom and thread on eight beads. Insert the needle back into the sphere at the same point to make a loop.

6 For the flower button, use a vanishing fabric pen to draw around the 3cm/1¼in self-cover button on to the silk. Draw another circle 1cm/½in larger and cut out. Mark five equally spaced points around the inner circle.

7 Thread a needle and fasten the thread at the centre of the circle. Thread on 20 large transparent glass beads, then insert the needle back at the same point to make a loop.

8 Bring the needle out at one of the points marked on the circle. Couch down the loop at this point with a stitch between the tenth and eleventh beads. Make four more glass-bead petals in the same way.

9 Stitch a green crystal bead in the centre of the flower.

10 Run a gathering stitch 3mm/⅛in from the raw edge. Place the self-cover button in the centre of the silk and pull up the gathering thread. Secure with a few small stitches and attach the back of the button.

▶

11 For the tassel button, draw around a 1.5cm/⅝in self-cover button on to a piece of taffeta, then draw another circle 7mm/⅜in larger and cut out. Thread a needle and fasten the thread in the centre of the circle. Thread on a green glass bead and eight copper beads, then pass the needle back through the green bead and fasten off. Gather the raw edges and cover the button as in step 10.

12 For the jewel-encrusted button, draw around a 1.5cm/⅝in self-cover button on to a piece of taffeta, then draw another circle 7mm/⅜in larger and cut out. Run a gathering stitch around the edge and cover the button as in step 10. Thread a needle and fasten the thread in the centre of the button. Thread on a green crystal bead and some small transparent glass beads, then pass the needle back through the green bead. Make another stitch and repeat until the button is completely covered.

These richly decorative earrings are made of card tubes covered in velvet ribbon then wrapped with metallic thread and gold wire studded with beads. All the larger beads are attached with hatpins.

Wrapped Earrings

you will need
thin card (stock)
pencil and ruler
scissors
velvet ribbon, 5cm/2in wide
needle and matching sewing thread
red metallic embroidery thread
textured gold wire
wire cutters
beading needle
matching beading thread
small green glass beads
4 hatpins
8 x 4mm/³⁄₁₆in brass flower beads
8 x 6mm/⁵⁄₁₆in red glass beads
12 x 4mm/³⁄₁₆in red glass beads
round-nosed (snub-nosed) pliers
4 x 7mm/³⁄₈in hexagonal brass beads
silver earring wires

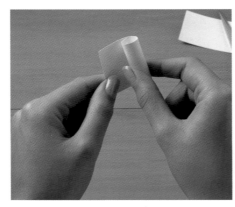

1 Cut two 4 x 7cm/1½ x 2¾in rectangles of card. Starting from one short side, roll each into a narrow tube 1.5cm/⅝in in diameter.

2 Cut two pieces of velvet ribbon 6 cm/2½in long. Roll a piece of ribbon around each card tube, right side out.

3 Fold under the raw edges of the ribbon and slip-stitch the seam. Thread a needle with red metallic thread, double it and knot the end. Fasten it to the end of a tube, wrap it evenly up the tube to the other end and fasten off.

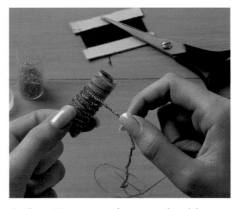

4 Cut 40 pieces of textured gold wire, each 1.5cm/⅝in long. Thread a beading needle with beading thread and fasten to the end of a tube. Thread on pieces of gold wire and small green glass beads alternately. Wrap the beaded thread around the tube between the strands of metallic thread and fasten off at the other end. Wrap the second tube to match.

5 Push a hatpin through each tube 5mm/¼in from the top so that the ends are of an equal length each side. Thread a flower bead, a large red bead and three small red beads on to each side. Twist the ends into spirals, snipping off the excess if necessary.

6 Taking another hatpin for each tube, thread on a brass bead, a large red bead, a hexagonal bead, the wrapped tube, then the same beads in reverse. Trim each hatpin end and bend into a loop. Attach earring wires to the top loops.

Inspired by the designs of the Art Deco movement, the geometric pattern of this bracelet is worked in pearlized ice-cream colours. The piece is worked in small glass beads on a bead loom.

Woven Bracelet

you will need

tape measure

beading thread

scissors

bead loom

beading needle

beeswax

small light green, pink, grey and purple glass beads

adhesive tape

wool lining fabric

needle and matching sewing thread

3 buttons with shanks

1 Measure your wrist to determine the length of the bracelet and add an extra 45cm/18in. Cut 21 warp threads to the total length. Lay out the threads and knot together at one end. Divide evenly into two strands. Slip the knot over the roller rivets of the beading loom. Wind on the threads a little by turning the roller, then spread the threads out and arrange one in each coil of the spring.

2 Tie a knot in the other end of the warp threads. Slip this over the rivet in the other roller with approximately half the threads on each side as before, and wind on. Arrange the threads in the corresponding coils of the other spring and wind the rollers on to adjust the tension – the warp threads should be taut.

3 Thread a beading needle with a long thread and draw the thread through beeswax. Tie the end of the thread to the far left warp thread 2.5cm/1in from the roller. Thread on 20 beads, pushing them up as far as they will go and fitting them between the warp threads.

4 Push the beads up through the spaces between the warp threads, and pass the needle back through the beads above the threads. Pull the thread tight. Thread on 20 more beads and repeat.

5 Continue, following the pattern at the back of the book. When complete, finish off the weaving by passing the needle back through several rows of beads. Tie a knot and trim the thread.

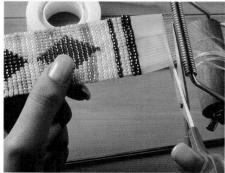

6 To remove the work from the loom, cut two lengths of adhesive tape and stick them firmly over the unbeaded warp threads at either end of the work. Cut the threads near the spring.

7 Cut a piece of wool lining fabric to the same size as the finished work. Tuck the free warp threads under and assemble the work and the lining with the wrong sides together. Now work a slip stitch all around the finished piece.

8 On one end of the bracelet, stitch three buttons at equal distances. Make three beaded loops in corresponding positions at the other end, large enough to fit over the buttons.

We tend to think that Victorian colours were always dark and sombre, but this beautiful embroidered and beaded jewellery was reproduced from original 19th-century pieces displayed in a costume museum.

Victorian Earrings and Brooch

you will need

tracing paper, pencil, card (stock) and
scissors (for templates)
30cm/12in square cream cotton fabric
embroidery hoop
needle and matching sewing thread
stranded embroidery thread (floss) in
pale green and warm pink
invisible thread
beading needle
tiny crystal beads
iron
30cm/12in square fusible interfacing
30cm/12in square satin lining
small scissors for cutting fabric
brooch back
earring wires

1 Copy the templates provided at the back of the book and then transfer the designs to your cream cotton fabric. Fit the cotton material into an embroidery hoop. Begin embroidering the brooch shape at the outer edge. Using three strands of green thread, work four rows of chain stitch. Work three rows in pink thread, followed by four more rows in green.

2 Fill the centre of the brooch with beads. Now iron the interfacing on to the wrong side of the satin lining and use the template to mark out the shape of the brooch.

▲ **3** Cut out the brooch and the lining, with a 1cm/½in seam allowance around each piece. Trim the corners, snip the curves and turn in the edges. Slip-stitch the backing to the embroidery.

4 Sew a loop of five beads on to each point of the brooch using a double thread, and finish off securely. Stitch on the brooch back.

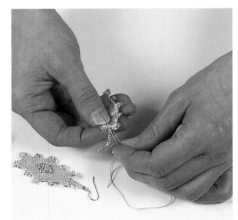

5 Make the earrings in the same way, but add extra loops of beads in between the points. At the top of the earrings thread on four beads and an earring hook and bring the thread back through the beads before finishing off securely.

Typically Victorian, this butterfly decoration would look most elegant on a simple black dress. It could also be pinned to a belt in the place of a buckle, or even used as a hair ornament for a special occasion.

Butterfly Brooch

you will need

20cm/8in square closely woven black fabric

vanishing fabric pen

embroidery hoop

beading needle and black sewing thread

scissors

20cm/8in square black felt

mounting (mat) board

double-sided tape

large round iridescent beads

large and small long black beads

large and small round black beads

craft (utility) knife

cutting board

latex adhesive

brooch back

1 Transfer the butterfly design provided with the templates at the back of the book on to the black fabric using a fabric pen, and fit the material into an embroidery hoop. Thread the needle with a double thread and knot the end.

3 Cut out the butterfly, leaving a 1cm/½in border. Trim the corners and snip into the curves. Using the template, cut butterfly shapes from felt and mounting board. Score down each side of the body on the board. Cut double-sided tape to fit round the edge and stretch the beaded fabric on to the board.

2 Sew on the large round, iridescent beads individually to make the eyes and highlights of the wings. Outline the body with large long beads and the wings with shorter beads, then fill in the rest of the butterfly with small round beads.

4 Use latex adhesive to glue the felt shape on to the back of the butterfly. When dry, stitch bead feelers on to the head: take the needle though a long bead, then a round bead, then back through the long bead on each side. Stitch the brooch fastening on to the back. Now gently bend the wings forward.

Buttons can easily be made from all sorts of shells, as long as there is a means of attaching them. They look especially effective on clothing made from natural fabrics, such as wool and cotton, in neutral colours.

Snail-shell Buttons

you will need

protective gloves

epoxy putty

small snail shells

small eyelet screws

wire cutters

file or abrasive paper

needle and matching button thread

1 Wearing protective gloves, mix together the two parts of the epoxy putty. Push putty into the mouth of each snail shell and fill the spiral recesses on the back of the shell. Smooth the surface with your finger.

2 Press a small eyelet screw into the putty on the back of each shell. If the screw is too long for the depth of the shell, snip off the end with wire cutters before inserting it.

3 Leave the putty to dry, then file or sand smooth, making sure there are no sharp edges at the mouth of the shell. Sew the shell buttons on to the garment with a needle and matching button thread.

Combine the contemporary look of corrugated cardboard with a dynamic shell arrangement. For the finishing touch, paint the box in pure white, and the result is a seashell box that resembles a meringue-topped cake.

Seashell Jewellery Box

you will need

selection of seashells

round corrugated cardboard box
with lid

glue gun

paintbrush

white acrylic gesso or paint

1 Sort the seashells into different shapes and sizes. Arrange them on the lid of the box, using some larger shells as the bottom layer of the design.

2 When you are happy with the arrangement, begin to glue the bottom layer on. Glue the outside shells first, and gradually move inwards.

3 Work with the shell forms, building the middle of the design up into a domed shape.

4 Paint the box and the lid white. If you are using acrylic gesso, two coats will give a good matt (flat) covering; ordinary acrylic paint will benefit from an extra coat.

Rainbow cockle shells in pretty, variegated colours are stitched on to a coloured cord to make this simple necklace. The long trimmed ties at the back make it a perfect accessory for beachwear or a backless dress.

Cockle-shell Necklace

you will need

rainbow cockle (small clam) shells

coloured cord

reusable putty adhesive

mini-drill

file

stranded embroidery thread (floss)

embroidery needle

epoxy resin glue

2 small winkle shells

1 Select an odd number of cockle shells and arrange them around the cord with the largest one in the centre at the front of the necklace.

2 Supporting each shell on a lump of reusable putty adhesive, drill a small hole through the top. File any rough edges smooth.

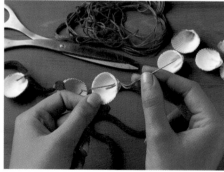

3 Stitch the shells on to the cord using embroidery thread.

4 Apply epoxy resin glue to the ends of the cord and insert each one into a small winkle shell.

The shell used to make this romantic locket is called a heart cockle because of its shape. It opens naturally down the middle, revealing a chamber large enough to conceal a message or small memento.

Valentine's Locket

1 Holding the shell steady on a piece of reusable putty adhesive, drill a small hole through the top of each half through which to thread the ribbon.

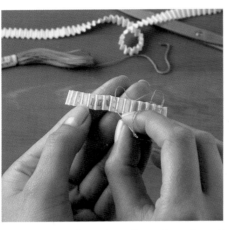

2 Using pink embroidery thread and an embroidery needle, stitch the words "I love you" inside the pleats of a small piece of pleated satin ribbon.

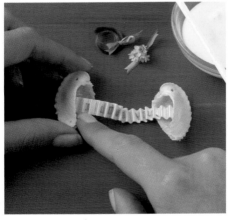

3 Glue one end of the ribbon inside each half of the cockle shell and leave to dry. Tuck the ribbon inside and insert small mementoes such as a lock of hair and a photograph.

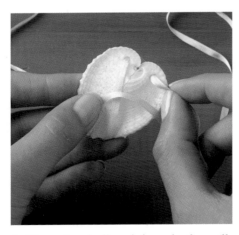

4 Close the shell and thread a fine silk ribbon through the holes at the top of the shell. Wrap the ribbon around the shell to hold it closed.

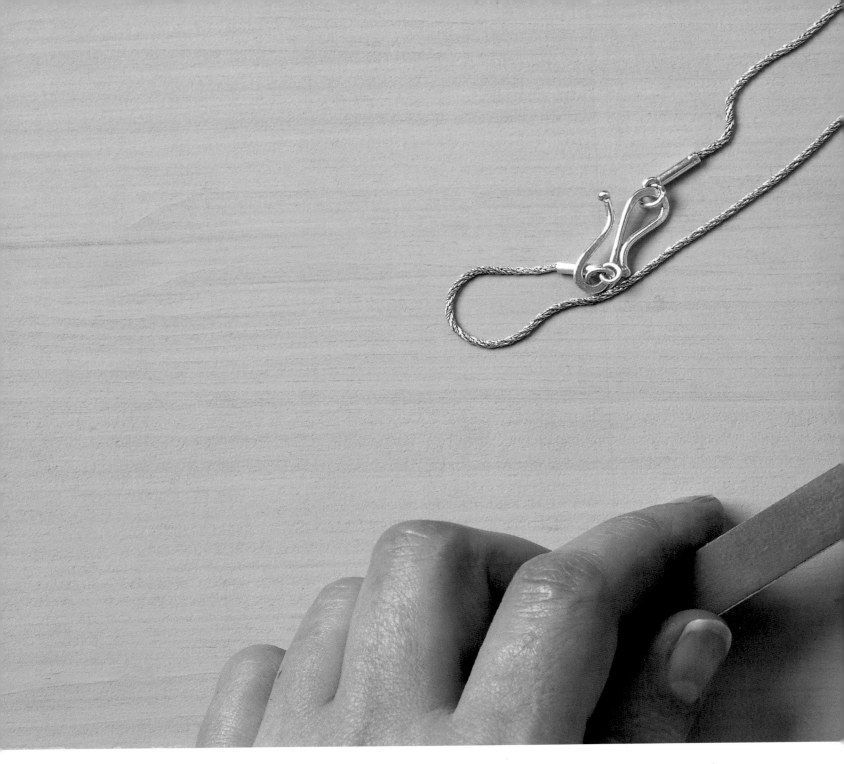

Enamelling and Metalwork

As soon as early people learnt how to work metal, they valued it as much for its beauty as its practical uses: the creation of jewellery, from delicate silver filigree to magical iron rings, has been an important skill in every civilization. Enamelling also has a long history of decorative use and early craftsmen used it in jewellery to imitate precious stones. Learning to use these materials in new designs continues a beautiful art and an ancient tradition.

Enamel is a form of glass and enamelling is the process of fusing it to metal using heat. Most materials need to be obtained from a specialist supplier: start by buying what you need for the simplest projects.

Enamelling Materials

Acids and pickles

Dilute solutions of various acids are used to degrease and de-oxidize metal before or after firing.

Ceramic fibre

This can be moulded to support awkwardly shaped pieces during firing.

Enamels

Jewellery enamels are available in lump or powder form, with or without lead. Leaded and lead-free enamels cannot be used together. Use transparent, translucent or opaque enamels to create different effects.

Enamel gum solution

Various organic gum solutions are available, some as sprays. Dilute solution is used to position cloisonné wires; a weak solution is used to

hold powder enamel before firing. Use sparingly.

Etchants

Solutions of nitric and other acids are painted on metal to produce etched designs for filling with enamel.

Foil

Fine gold (23.5 ct) and silver (.995 ct) foil are available in a variety of thicknesses. Gold leaf is usually too thin for enamelling purposes.

Kaolin (ballclay, batwash)

This helps prevent enamel adhering to the firing support or the kiln floor.

Mica

In the technique called *plique-à-jour*, "windows" of translucent enamel are created in a pierced metal form. A

sheet of mica can be used to support the enamel when firing such items.

Pumice powder

A pumice and water paste is used to polish enamel and metal after firing.

Resists

Stopping-out varnish can be painted on to areas of metal to be protected during etching. PnP blue acetate film produces a photographic resist.

Sheet metal

Copper and silver sheets come in various thicknesses and sections. Silver should be at least .925 (Sterling) quality. Avoid beryllium-containing copper.

Solder

Hard (4N, "IT" grade) silver solder should be used prior to enamelling.

Washing (baking) soda crystals

Use a soda solution to neutralize acids.

Water

In hard-water areas use bottled water or rainwater, as limescale and additives can impair the clarity of enamels.

Wire

Copper, fine silver and fine gold wire are available in rectangular section, pre-annealed, for cloisonné.

The main piece of equipment needed for enamelling is a domestic-sized gas or electric kiln. This and other specialist items are available from enamellers' and jewellers' suppliers.

Enamelling Equipment

Artist's brushes
Pure sable paintbrushes are the traditional tools for applying wet enamel.

Brass brush
Use a suede or other brass brush to clean metal after pickling.

Diamond-impregnated paper
This is a cleaner and faster abrasive than carborundum, the traditional abrasive for enamel, and is invaluable for concave surfaces.

Doming block, swage block, mandrel and punches
These blocks of steel, brass or hardwood are used to shape metal. Use a hammer with steel and brass blocks and a mallet with wood.

Felt polishing mop
Impregnated with pumice powder and water, a felt mop is used to polish fired enamel, either by hand or connected to an electric polishing motor.

Files
Use hand files to remove burrs after cutting metal. Diamond files can be used with water to abrade fired enamel.

Glass fibre brush
This will not scratch metal and can be used to clean enamel. Avoid contact with the hands.

Kiln
Electric kilns take longer to heat up to firing temperature than gas-fired kilns but are comparatively inexpensive. A regulator (thermostat) is needed to prevent overheating and a pyrometer gives an accurate temperature reading. Use ready-made firing supports or make them from stainless-steel mesh.

Pestle and mortar
Use only vitrified porcelain to grind and wash enamels.

Quills
Goose quills, from calligraphers' suppliers, are used to apply wet enamel.

Rolling mill
Use to impress textured designs on sheet silver for *champlevé* enamel.

Sieves (strainers)
Use to apply dry enamel. Match the size of the mesh to that of the ground enamel fragments.

Soldering equipment
You need solder, charcoal, a gas blowtorch and borax-based flux (auflux).

Tongs and tweezers
Brass or plastic tongs or tweezers must be used to move metal in and out of pickle or etchants.

Enamelling involves high temperatures and hazardous substances. Work in a well-ventilated place, wear protective clothing, follow all manufacturers' instructions and turn off the kiln when not needed.

Enamelling Techniques

Preparation of Metal

Metal must be degreased and de-oxidized (pickled) before enamelling. To make it more malleable, anneal it by heating with a blowtorch to cherry-red. Allow it to return to black then quench in cold water and pickle to remove oxidation.

1 To degrease, abrade metal with emery paper. Treat copper by placing in a general pickle solution (a 10% solution of sulphuric acid, safety pickle or alum).

2 Cover sterling or Britannia silver in neat nitric acid and swill gently until the metal appears white. (Fine silver does not need de-oxidizing.)

3 Brighten all metals with a brass brush and washing-up liquid (liquid soap) solution. Dry on a clean cotton cloth, taking care not to touch the area to be enamelled with your fingers.

Soldering

When designing a piece, aim to have as little soldering as possible under enamelling, to avoid the enamel discolouring or bubbling. During soldering, support the work with binding wire or tweezers if necessary, so that the sections do not move while you work.

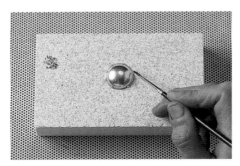

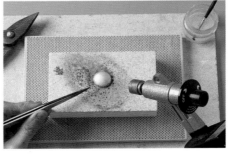

1 Apply borax-based flux (auflux) to the joint. Cut a length of solder into small pieces and apply them to the joint using a brush laden with flux.

2 Play a flame over the whole piece to dry the flux without letting it bubble. When it is crystalline, direct the flame on the joint to heat both sides evenly until the solder melts.

3 Cool the piece then immerse in general pickle solution to remove fire stain and flux. Rinse the metal under running water, dry and remove any excess solder using a file.

Acid Etching

After metal has been pickled and brightened, the surface can be etched ready to take enamel. Wear protective gloves and goggles when working with etchants, and use only brass or plastic tweezers.

1 To protect the back and edges of the prepared metal from the etchant, paint on three coats of stopping-out varnish. Leave to dry.

2 Paint the design on the front in varnish. The acid will etch away any areas that are not covered by varnish. Alternatively, cover the whole surface then remove the varnish from areas to be etched using a fine steel point.

3 Place the piece in a solution of 1 part neat nitric acid to 3 parts cold water in an open plastic container. Stroke away bubbles using a feather. Remove the piece when the required depth of etching is achieved (not more than one-third of the thickness of the metal).

4 Rinse the metal under running water, using a glass fibre brush to clean off the etchant. Remove any remaining varnish with brush cleaner and brighten the surface by cleaning with a brass brush and washing-up liquid (liquid soap) solution.

Photo-etching

Instead of painting the design on the metal, you can create a resist photographically. Draw a high-contrast black and white design, twice final size, with all lines at least 0.7mm/0.03in thick. (The black areas represent the metal and the white the enamelled areas.) Reduce the design to actual size on a photocopier.

Photocopy the reduced image at high contrast on a sheet of PnP blue acetate film, emulsion side up. Iron the resist on to the prepared metal, using a cotton/dry iron setting, to fix the image. Paint the back and edges of the piece with stopping-out varnish and etch with nitric acid as above.

Preparing Enamel

Intricate designs and curved surfaces usually require the enamel to be more finely ground than large, flat pieces. To start, break up enamel nuggets by wrapping them in a cotton cloth and hitting with a hammer.

1 In a clean mortar, cover a small piece of enamel with purified water and hit it with the pestle until it resembles granulated sugar. Add another piece and repeat until you have enough for your project, adding water to cover if necessary.

2 Hold the pestle upright and grind firmly with a circular action until the enamel feels soft and powdery. Allow to settle, then pour off the water. Rinse until the water runs clear and the enamel is uniform in colour.

Wet Application of Enamel

Pour the rinsed enamel into a palette and keep covered with water. It should be applied in several thin layers rather than one thick one, using a fine artist's brush, goose quill or stainless-steel point.

1 Pour off excess water and tip the palette so the waterline lies across the enamel. Pick up the enamel from just above the water. Apply evenly to the metal, pushing it well into any corners as it will draw back during firing.

2 Draw off any excess water by touching the edge of the metal with a clean cotton cloth. Do not touch the enamel itself as this will impair the finish of the fired surface. Fire the piece as soon as possible.

Dry Application of Enamel

Once the enamel is ground and cleaned, pour off as much water as possible then spread the paste on cooking foil, cover and leave to dry on top of the kiln or a radiator.

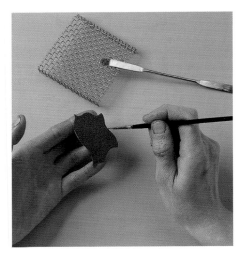

1 Having prepared the metal by degreasing and de-oxidizing it, cover the area to be enamelled with a layer of enamel gum, applying it thinly with a brush. Place it on a sheet of paper.

2 Place the enamel powder in a sieve (strainer), hold it about 5cm/2in above the metal and tap gently. Lift the metal and clean any excess enamel from the sides with a fine brush. Place the piece on a trivet ready for firing.

3 On subsequent layers, if you wish, you can paint a design in the enamel gum, or use a stencil, before sifting the enamel. Alternatively, you can scratch a design in the enamel before firing, using a paintbrush or steel point.

Kiln Firing   The temperature of the kiln should be about 900°C/1,650°F for small items. Place the piece to be fired near the kiln to remove any moisture. Put it in the kiln when the surface looks crystalline and no more steam rises.

1 The enamel will lighten when it is first placed in the kiln and the metal will oxidize. Later the enamel will darken, still appearing matt (flat) and granular.

2 The enamel will then start to melt and look uneven but shiny.

3 Fully fired enamel looks smooth and shiny. If it pulls away from the edges and discolours, then it is overfired. It is best to underfire the first layers slightly and keep the highest firing for the last.

Finishing   In order to achieve a smooth finish, the enamel needs to be abraded and polished after it has been fired. Depending on the shape of the piece you can use carborundum stones, diamond-impregnated paper or silicon carbide (wet and dry) paper, all of which are readily available in a range of grades.

1 Abrade the enamel using plenty of water and working in all directions. The surface will appear matt, showing up any low spots that may need to be filled with enamel and re-fired. Remove the residue with a glass fibre brush and water. Dry with a cotton cloth and do not touch the surface.

2 Re-fire the piece. When it is cool, place in a general pickle solution. Polish the enamel and metal with a paste of pumice powder and water, using a felt polishing mop either by hand or using a polishing motor running at 900–1200 rpm.

Fine wire and metal foils can be obtained from craft suppliers as well as hardware stores, but look out for containers such as oil cans and other unusual sources of metal that you can recycle.

Sheet Metal and Wirework Materials

Brass shim

Thin brass sheet is available in a range of thicknesses, as flat sheets or in rolls.

Copper wire

Soft copper wire has an attractive, warm colour and is easy to work with. It is available in a wide range of gauges and different tempers (hardnesses).

Galvanized wire

A coating of zinc on steel wire prevents it rusting. Galvanized wire is springy and fairly hard to bend in thicker gauges.

Paints

Use hardwearing enamel paints to add bright, opaque colours to pieces of metal jewellery.

Pipe cleaners and paper clips (fasteners)

These quirky wire products are fun to work with. Both are available in many different colours and styles.

Silver-plated copper wire

This pretty wire is particularly well suited to jewellery making.

Solder

This is designed to melt and then harden to form a joint between pieces of metal. You should therefore always use a solder that has a lower melting point than the metals you are joining, and various alloys are available.

Tin plate

This is mild sheet steel coated with tin to stop it tarnishing. Biscuit tins are a useful source of recycled tin plate.

Wired tape

This thin, flat plastic tape with a wire core is designed for household and garden use and is available in various colours, such as green for tying plants.

Zinc sheet

Thin zinc sheet has a matt (flat) surface and is fairly soft and easy to cut.

Epoxy resin glue

Strong, two-part glue can be used to join small sections of metal and items such as brooch backs.

You may already have many of the tools you will need as they are fairly basic. For coiling and shaping wire accurately it is essential to invest in some good pliers.

Sheet Metal and Wirework Equipment

Bench vice

Use a vice to clamp pieces of metal to a workbench or table when filing, drilling and hammering edges.

Centre punch

Use a punch or nail (with a hammer) to make decorative holes in metal.

File

A hand file can be used to remove burrs of metal from the edges after cutting out a shape from sheet metal.

Hammer

A medium ball hammer is used with a punch or nail to decorate tin plate, or alone to create a hammered texture.

Pliers

Use round-nosed (snub-nosed) or half-round pliers to coil wire, and parallel (channel-type) pliers to flatten coils.

Protective clothes

Heavyweight gloves and a thick work shirt should always be worn when working with metal.

Silicon carbide (wet and dry) paper

Damp fine-grade paper is good for finishing filed metal edges. Wrap the paper around a small wooden block.

Soldering iron

A soldering iron is used to heat solder when joining pieces of metal. The job should always be done on a fireproof soldering mat.

Tin snips

These are very strong shears, designed especially for cutting metal. They are available with either straight or curved blades (the latter type are used to cut curves and circles more easily).

Wire cutters

Always choose wire cutters that have good leverage. Don't be tempted to use scissors to cut wire as it will ruin their blades.

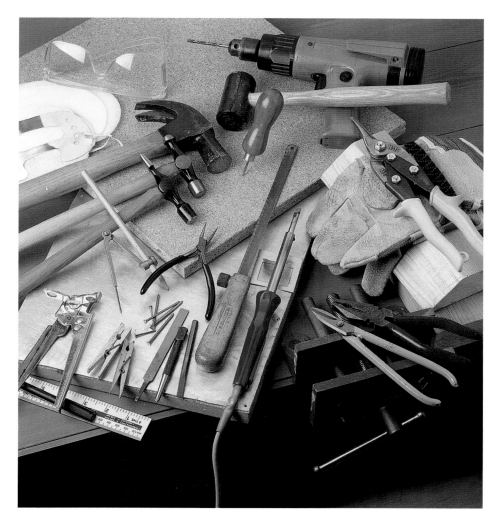

Neat wire coils and twists will make all the difference to the appearance of your finished pieces. Practise on a few spare lengths of wire to get the feel of your tools and the tension required.

Wirework Techniques

Making Coils   The coil is the most commonly used decorative device in wirework. If you are making a symmetrical ornament it will take some practice to create open coils of matching sizes.

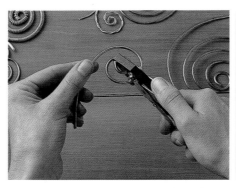

1 Using a pair of round-nosed (snub-nosed) pliers, make a small loop at the end of the wire. Hold the loop in the pliers, place your thumb against the wire and draw the wire across it to form a curve. Hold the pliers still and use your thumb to supply the tension needed as you bend the wire down.

2 After the first round has been formed, hold the middle of the coil flat with parallel (channel-type) pliers and continue to pull the wire round in a curve with your other hand. Use your eye to judge the space between the remaining turns of the coil.

3 Begin a closed coil in the same way as an open coil, by making a small loop in the end of the wire.

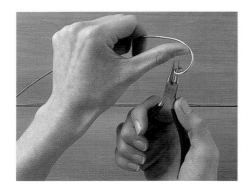

Twisting Soft Wire   A hand drill can be used to twist soft wire neatly and quickly. You can use wires with different finishes and twist multiple strands in this way.

4 Hold the loop securely with parallel pliers and keep bending the wire around it, adjusting the position of the pliers as you work, until the coil is the required size.

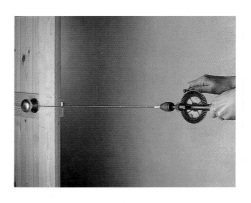

◀ Double the length of wire and loop it around a door handle. Wrap the ends in masking tape and secure them in the chuck of the drill. Keep the wire taut as you rotate the drill. Start slowly so that you can gauge the tension needed and continue until the wire is twisted to the degree required.

Thin sheet metal is not difficult to work with but the edges can be sharp, and tools such as tin snips and soldering irons should be treated with respect. Always wear protective clothing, even for small projects.

Sheet Metal Techniques

Cutting Metal

The cutting of any sheet metal produces small razor-sharp shards. Collect up these scraps as you go and keep them all together so that you can dispose of them safely when you have finished.

1 To avoid creating jagged edges, never close the blades of the shears completely. Keep the blades in the cut until the line is complete.

2 When cutting a curved shape, don't attempt to turn tin shears or snips: cut as much as you can then turn the metal to continue.

3 Large cans provide an excellent source of tin plate. Use a hacksaw blade to make a cut just below the top so that you are able to insert a blade of the tin snips and then cut around the drum. Cut straight down the side, then around the base, pushing back the panel as you go.

Finishing Edges

The cut edges of a piece of sheet metal are very sharp and should be smoothed immediately to prevent them causing harm to you or anyone else.

1 Small shapes should be firmly clamped in a vice for filing. Smooth all edges using a hand file, moving the file forwards at a right angle to the metal in one light stroke, then lifting it to repeat.

2 After the rough edges have been filed, make them completely smooth by finishing with fine-grade silicon carbide (wet and dry) paper. Dampen the paper and wrap it around a small sanding block.

This stylized – and stylish – bird, who carries a heart in his beak, is enamelled on silver to make an attractive lapel pin. In this project, the opaque enamel colours create a matt (flat) surface.

Bird Lapel Pin

you will need

tracing paper and pencil

double-sided tape

16 gauge/1.3mm/0.05in silver sheet

piercing saw

drill

silver tube and wire (inner diameter of tube to match thickness of wire)

soldering equipment

hard solder

pliers

burnisher

pestle and mortar

opaque enamels: white, bright red and mid-blue

black transparent enamel

enamel gum

glass fibre brush

trivet

fine artist's brush or quill

kiln and firing equipment

diamond-impregnated paper

fine-grade silicon carbide (wet and dry) paper

nail buffer

epoxy resin glue

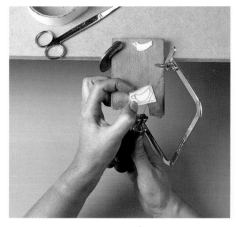

1 Trace the template at the back of the book. Stick the tracing on to the silver sheet using double-sided tape and cut out with a piercing saw. Drill a hole so that you can thread the saw blade through to reach the area between the heart and the bird.

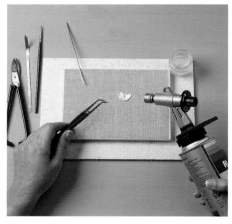

2 Cut and file a piece of silver tube 5mm/¼in long. Solder it in an upright position on to the back, using hard solder. For the pin, cut a 6cm/2½in length of silver wire. Bend with pliers 5mm/¼in in from one end to make a right angle.

3 Burnish the edges of the bird to provide a "grip" for the enamel to adhere to. Grind and clean the enamels then add a drop of enamel gum to each and water to cover.

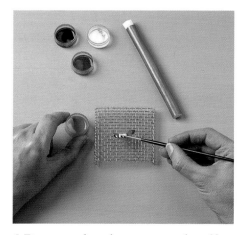

4 Degrease the silver using a glass fibre brush and water. Place the bird on a trivet and apply the enamel using a paintbrush or quill.

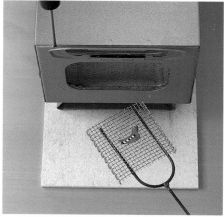

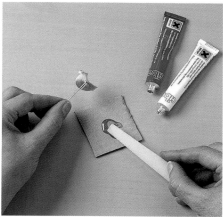

5 Place the bird on top of the kiln to dry, then fire it. Apply two more layers of enamel, firing each layer.

6 Abrade the enamel with diamond-impregnated paper and water. Smooth with damp silicon carbide paper and rinse. Leave the enamel surface matt (flat). Buff the plain silver side of the bird. Glue the pin into the tube using epoxy resin glue.

Make a set of these wonderful buttons in any size, to suit a special garment. They are decorated with a delicate scattering of tiny gold or silver shapes and dabs of brightly coloured enamel.

Multicoloured Buttons

you will need

drill

20 gauge/0.8mm/0.03in copper discs, size as required

pumice powder

toothbrush

pestle and mortar

enamel gum

artist's brushes

sieve (strainer)

opaque enamels in various colours

kiln and firing equipment

stilts to fit buttons

scissors

flat gold or silver *cloisonné* wire

hole punch

34 gauge/0.16mm/0.006in silver sheet

1 Drill two large holes side by side in the centre of each copper disc.

2 Clean the copper with pumice powder and water, using a toothbrush.

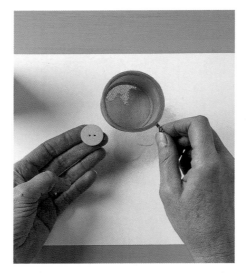

3 Grind and clean the enamels. Lightly apply enamel gum to the back of each button. Using a sieve, apply enamel, using different colours. Leave to dry, then fire in the kiln. Clean the fronts and repeat, supporting the buttons on stilts. Apply a second layer of enamel if necessary.

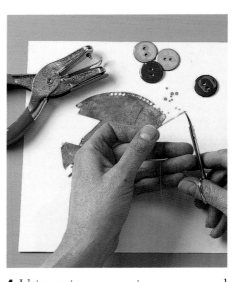

4 Using scissors, cut tiny squares and triangles off the end of the gold or silver wire. Punch holes in the silver sheet to make tiny circles.

5 Decorate the buttons with the metal shapes, secured with enamel gum. Moisten a little enamel powder with enamel gum to make a paste, then apply to the buttons in small dots using a fine paintbrush.

6 Support the buttons on stilts and fire in the kiln until the enamel dots have fused. When cool, remove oxidation by cleaning with pumice powder and water, using a toothbrush.

Embellish a variety of enamelled silver beads with tiny scraps of gold foil for a really opulent effect. Instead of a chain, you could thread a few beads on to a leather thong or a silk cord.

Gold Foil Beads

you will need

selection of silver beads

18 gauge/1mm/0.04in silver wire

scissors

metal rod of diameter to match holes in beads

piercing saw

soldering equipment

hard solder

pliers

glass fibre brush

trivet

pestle and mortar

turquoise transparent enamel

enamel gum

fine artist's paintbrush or quill

kiln and firing equipment

diamond-impregnated paper

gold foil

nail buffer

necklace chain

assorted silver and semi-precious beads

necklace findings and clasp

easy solder or epoxy resin glue

1 Assemble a collection of silver beads in different shapes and sizes to add interest to the necklace.

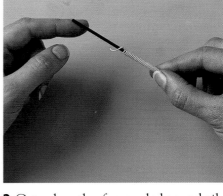

2 Cut a length of annealed round silver wire. Spiral it around a metal rod of the same diameter as the holes in the beads.

3 Remove the rod then cut down the length of the spiral, using a piercing saw, to make jump rings. Bend the rings to close the join and solder with hard solder.

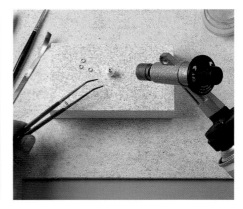

4 Using hard solder, solder a jump ring around the hole at the top and bottom of each bead. Remove the firestain and rinse, then clean the beads with a glass fibre brush and water.

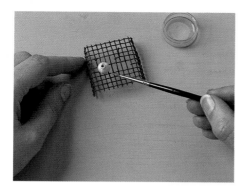  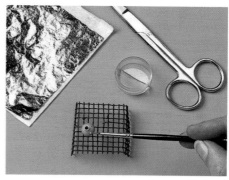

5 Cut and bend a piece of wire up from the trivet and place a bead on it to hold it during enamelling. Grind and clean the enamel then add a few drops of enamel gum and water to cover. Using the wet enamel as dry as possible, apply it to the bead with a fine paintbrush or quill. Dry out the enamelled beads on top of the kiln.

6 Fire the beads in the kiln. Repeat with two more layers of enamel, firing each layer. Abrade the enamel smooth with diamond-impregnated paper and water. Rinse.

7 Cut up small pieces of gold foil into geometric shapes with a pair of sharp scissors. Now, using a fine paintbrush dipped in a little enamel gum, attach these pieces of foil to some of the enamelled beads. Dry on top of the kiln and then fire.

8 Polish the silver edges of the beads with a nail buffer. Thread on to the chain, mixing the enamelled beads with plain silver and semi-precious beads.

9 Attach the findings to the chain using easy solder. Solder or glue on the clasp. The clasp can be glued if using a leather thong or silk cord.

The subtle etched design resembling snakeskin on this handsome ring is enamelled in two shades of grey. Engrave a matching design around the side. The dimensions given here will make a medium to large ring.

Reptilian Ring

you will need

half-round jeweller's pliers

8.5mm/³⁄₈in x 5.8cm/2¼in strip of 12 gauge/2mm/0.08in silver, for the ring

soldering equipment

hard solder

general pickle solution

ring mandrel

mallet

file

emery paper

graver

17mm/²⁄₃in diameter circle of 18 gauge/1mm/0.04in silver, for the domed top

doming block

doming punch

drill

2mm/³⁄₃₂in x 6cm/2½in strip of 14 gauge/1.6mm/0.06in silver, for the bezel

2cm/³⁄₄in diameter circle of 18 gauge/1mm/0.04in silver, for the base

4mm/³⁄₁₆in square of 22 gauge/ 0.6mm/0.025in silver

14BA ³⁄₁₆th cheesehead brass screw and matching nut

stopping-out varnish

fine artist's paintbrush or quill

nitric acid

glass fibre brush

brush cleaner

brass brush

washing-up liquid (liquid soap)

easy solder

pumice powder

toothbrush

pestle and mortar

transparent enamels: mid-grey and dark grey

kiln and firing equipment

carborundum stone or diamond file

silicon carbide (wet and dry) paper

epoxy resin glue

1 Using half-round-nosed pliers, bend the strip of 12 gauge silver into a ring smaller than the finger size. Solder the joint, using hard solder. Pickle and rinse.

2 Check that the ring is circular by placing it on the mandrel and correcting it with a mallet. File, then sandpaper inside and out.

3 File the sides parallel. Scribe a light centre guideline around the outside. With the joint at the top, file a taper on both sides from a width of 8.5mm/³⁄₈in at the bottom to 4mm/³⁄₁₆in at the top. Engrave a reptilian design around the outside, using a graver, or etch with acid.

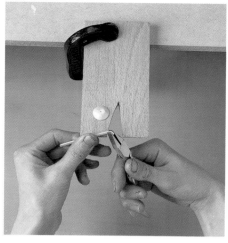

4 For the top, place the annealed 17mm/²/₃in silver circle in the doming block. Using a doming punch and a mallet, tap into a hemispherical shape.

5 Mark the centre of the domed top and drill a small hole to take the decorative brass screw.

6 Using the half-round-nosed pliers, bend the strip of 14 gauge silver into a collar, or bezel, so that it will fit snugly around the base of the domed top. Now solder the joint with hard solder. Check that the shape of the bezel is a circle on the ring mandrel, as described in step 2.

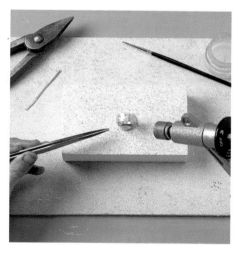

7 Solder the 2cm/³/₄in circle of silver to the bezel with hard solder to make the base. File the edge of the circle flush with the bezel, then file both to create an angled profile. Drill a 1mm hole through the centre of the 4mm/³/₁₆in silver square, then dome it to match the profile of the domed top. Thread the brass screw through the hole from the top and secure with hard solder underneath. File the top of the screw to make a decorative feature.

8 Clean and degrease the silver. Apply stopping-out varnish to the back, edges and hole of the domed top. Leave to dry, then paint a reptilian design in varnish on the front. Place in nitric acid diluted with 3 parts water for 3–3½ hours to etch the design. Rinse with water and a glass fibre brush and remove any remaining varnish with brush cleaner. Brighten the top using a brass brush and washing-up liquid solution.

9 Solder the bezel to the narrowest point of the ring strip at the joint, using easy solder. File and sand then apply pumice powder with a toothbrush. Brighten the silver with a glass fibre brush and washing-up liquid solution.

▶

10 Grind and clean the enamels. Wet-apply the mid-grey enamel to the entire top surface, checking that it does not run into the hole. Fire in the kiln and leave to cool. On the next three to four layers, emphasize the etched recesses with dark-grey enamel to suggest scales. Use mid-grey for the rest of the design.

11 Use a carborundum stone or dia-mond file and silicon carbide paper to abrade the enamel. Use a glass fibre brush to rinse under running water, then fire for the final time. When cool, scrub with a paste of pumice powder and a toothbrush. Thread the decorative brass screw through the central hole of the dome and secure using the 14BA nut. Glue into the bezel using epoxy resin glue.

Wet-applying enamel on round objects is easier if it is ground very finely and you control the amount of water carefully. For a frosted finish, place the beads in matting salts for 2–3 minutes before pickling.

Striped Necklace

you will need

dividers

50cm/20in length of thick-walled, silver joint tubing, 4mm/^{3}/16in diameter

square or triangular needle file or lathe

piercing saw with fine blade

tube cutter or pin vice

file

silicon carbide (wet and dry) paper

ball fraize

copper or silver wire

brass brush

washing-up liquid (liquid soap)

pestle and mortar

transparent enamels

stainless steel wire

fine artist's paintbrush or quill

clean cotton cloth

kiln and firing equipment

diamond file or carborundum stone

general pickle solution

nylon thread and beading needle or fine silver chain

co-ordinating beads (optional)

necklace clasp

1 Using dividers, mark unequal stripes at random along the silver tubing.

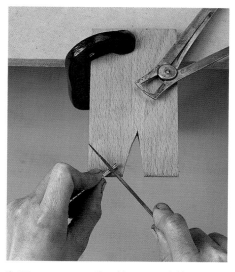

2 Using a needle file, carefully make straight-sided grooves around the circumference of the tubing to a depth of 0.3mm. Try to keep them as even in depth as possible. Alternatively, turn the grooves on a lathe.

3 Using a piercing saw, carefully cut off unequal lengths of silver tubing between the recesses to make the actual beads. ▶

4 File the ends of each bead and smooth with silicon carbide paper. Countersink the central hole of each bead using a ball fraize.

5 Temporarily thread several beads on to a loop of wire and scrub with a brass brush and washing-up liquid solution.

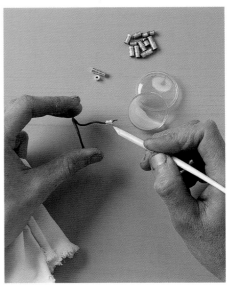

6 Grind the enamels very finely. Make several stainless-steel wire spirals to hold each bead firmly, as shown. Wet-apply the enamel, using a fine artist's paintbrush or quill. Draw off excess water with a clean cloth before firing.

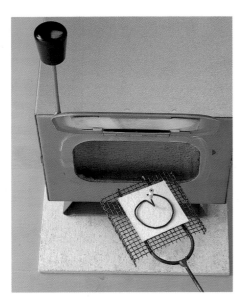

7 Keeping each bead on its wire spiral, fire in the kiln and leave to cool, still on the wire. Apply further layers of the same colour until each recess is full. Fire between each layer of enamel.

8 Thread each bead on a cranked length of stainless steel. Abrade each bead and smooth with silicon carbide paper, rotating the wired bead. Temporarily thread several beads on to a length of copper or silver wire. Rinse before and after pickling.

9 String the enamelled beads, perhaps interspersing them with co-ordinating beads. Alternatively, thread them on their own on to a fine silver chain. Attach a clasp.

Create your own design for these earrings, using transparent enamels in pale, clear colours. The holes should be large enough to allow the light to shine through but small enough to hold the wet enamel.

Plique-à-jour Earrings

you will need
pencil and paper
16 gauge/1.2mm/0.05in silver sheet
piercing saw
drill
tweezers
brass brush
washing-up liquid (liquid soap)
pestle and mortar
transparent enamels in pale colours
fine artist's paintbrush
trivet
kiln and firing equipment
sheet of mica (optional)
diamond-impregnated paper
pumice powder
jeweller's rouge
earring wires

1 Draw your design on paper and attach it to the silver sheet. Using a piercing saw, cut out the shapes. Drill holes where the enamel will appear, then insert the saw into each hole and cut out. Use the saw to smooth the edges from front and back.

2 Shape the silver with a pair of tweezers. Clean the silver with a brass brush and washing-up liquid solution. Grind and wash the transparent enamels.

3 Using a fine paintbrush, apply the wet enamel into the spaces in the earrings. Practise getting the right consistency – if the enamel is too wet, it will fall through the holes.

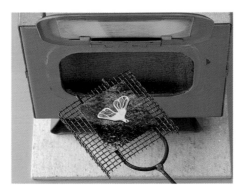

4 Fire while the enamel is still damp. Beginners may find it easier to fire on a sheet of mica. Remove from the kiln as soon as the enamel begins to melt. Refill the holes if the enamel has pulled to the side, and re-fire.

5 When the holes are completely filled, abrade the earrings with diamond-impregnated paper. Rinse and fire again. Polish with pumice powder and water, then jeweller's rouge. Attach the earring wires.

A central band of enamel with a simple photo-etched design makes an elegant decoration for this silver ring. You can omit the final firing if you would prefer a matt (flat) finish to the enamel.

Banded Ring

you will need

silver ring blank

PnP blue acetate film and iron

ring clamp

file

emery paper

pliers

binding wire

soldering equipment

hard solder

general pickle solution

ring mandrel

wooden or hide mallet

nitric acid

brass brush

washing-up liquid (liquid soap)

pestle and mortar

transparent enamels

enamel gum

fine artist's paintbrush

or quill

kiln and firing equipment

diamond-impregnated paper

pumice powder or felt

polishing mop

1 Photocopy the template provided at the back of the book to produce a high contrast black-and-white design for photo-etching on to the ring blank (see Enamelling Techniques section). Place the ring blank in a clamp and shorten it to the required finger size by filing the ends. Smooth the sides with a file and then emery paper.

2 Using a pair of pliers, carefully bend in the ends to form a ring. The shape doesn't need to be perfectly round at this stage. Now file the ends of the ring so that they will meet exactly and make a good joint.

3 Twist binding wire around the ring. Solder the joint with hard solder, then quench in cold water and dry. Remove the wire, then pickle the ring.

4 File off the excess solder. Place the ring on a ring mandrel and tap with a mallet until it is perfectly round. Remove firestain by placing the ring in nitric acid, and then rinse. Now, using a brass brush, brush the silver with water and washing-up liquid solution until it is shiny.

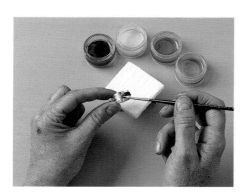

5 Grind and clean the enamels, then add a drop of enamel gum and water to cover. Apply carefully to the etched band using either a fine paintbrush or a quill. Leave the enamel to dry, then fire in the kiln. Now leave to cool.

6 Using medium-grade diamond-impregnated paper and water, abrade the enamel until you expose the silver design. Rinse the ring and apply more enamel to any shiny areas of the design then repeat the firing and abrading. Polish with fine-grade diamond-impregnated paper, rinse then fire again to glaze the surface if you wish. Leave to cool then pickle, rinse and polish the ring.

Choose transparent enamels in watery colours for these fish, set against a deep blue sea. The photo-etched design needs to be reversed for the second blank so that the cufflinks make a symmetrical pair.

Fishy Cufflinks

you will need

silver cufflink blanks to fit the template or 17 gauge/1.1mm/0.045in

silver sheet

PnP blue acetate film and iron

piercing saw

ring clamp

file

emery stick (board)

wooden doming block

wooden doming punch

mallet

nitric acid

brass brush

washing-up liquid (liquid soap)

pestle and mortar

transparent enamels

enamel gum

fine artist's paintbrush or quill

trivet

kiln and firing equipment

diamond-impregnated paper

emery paper

soldering equipment

easy solder

cufflink findings

general pickle solution

pumice powder or felt polishing mop

(optional)

1 Photocopy the template at the back of the book to produce a high contrast black-and-white design. This needs to be photo-etched on to the cufflink blanks or silver sheet (see Enamelling Techniques section). Cut out the cufflink shapes with a piercing saw, place each one in a clamp and file the edges straight. Polish the edges with a fine emery stick.

2 Place each cufflink in the doming block. Tap the silver with a doming punch and mallet to create the desired domed shape.

3 De-oxidize the silver by placing each piece in nitric acid for a few minutes and then rinsing in cold water. Using a brass brush, scrub with washing-up liquid solution until the metal is shiny.

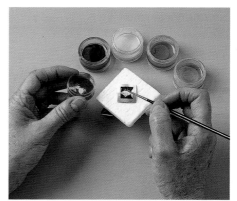

4 Grind and clean the enamels and add a drop of enamel gum to each. Apply the wet enamels to the design, using a paintbrush. Do not mix the colours. Leave to dry, then fire in the kiln until molten. Leave to cool.

5 Using a medium-grade diamond-impregnated paper and some water, abrade the enamel to expose the silver design, and then rinse. Apply more enamel and repeat. Polish with fine-grade paper, then fire again. Leave to cool. Remove the oxidation with emery paper.

6 Melt easy solder on to the foot of each finding and solder to the back of the cufflink. Cool, then pickle and polish the cufflinks.

The design for these jolly earrings is transferred to a pair of silver blanks using the photo-etching technique. Remember to apply it to the second earring in reverse so that the finished pieces are symmetrical.

Stargazer Earrings

you will need

silver earring blanks, to fit the template, or 17 gauge/1.1mm/0.045in

silver sheet

PnP blue acetate film and iron

piercing saw

ring clamp

file

fine emery stick (board)

masking tape

centre punch

drill

wooden doming block

wooden doming punch

mallet

nitric acid

brass brush

washing-up liquid (liquid soap)

pestle and mortar

transparent enamels

enamel gum

fine artist's paintbrush or quill

trivet

kiln and firing equipment

diamond-impregnated paper

emery paper

general pickle solution

pumice powder or felt polishing mop (optional)

earring wires

pliers

◀ **1** Photocopy the template provided at the back of the book to produce a high contrast black-and-white design the size of the finished earrings. This design needs to be photo-etched on to the earring blanks or silver sheet (see Enamelling Techniques section). Now cut out the earring shapes with a piercing saw, place each earring in a clamp and file the edges straight.

2 Polish the edges of the earrings with a fine emery stick to remove any scratch marks left after filing.

3 Secure each earring in turn on your work surface with masking tape. Centre punch and drill a hole in the top edge for the wires.

4 Place each earring in the doming block. Tap the silver with a doming punch and mallet to create the desired domed shape.

5 De-oxidize the earrings by placing them in nitric acid for a few minutes, then rinsing in cold water. Using a brass brush, brush with washing-up liquid solution until shiny. Hold by the edges only.

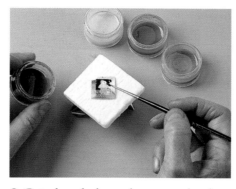

6 Grind and clean the enamels, then add a drop of enamel gum and water to cover. Apply the wet enamels, using a paintbrush or quill. Take care not to mix the colours.

7 Leave the earrings to dry, then fire in the kiln until the enamel is molten. Leave to cool. Apply further layers of enamel and fire each time until the cells of the design appear full.

8 Using medium-grade diamond-impregnated paper and water, abrade the enamel until you expose the silver design. Apply more enamel to any shiny areas, then repeat the firing, abrading and rinsing. Refire to glaze the surface.

9 Leave to cool. Abrade the back of the earrings with emery paper, and then place in pickle solution to remove oxidation.

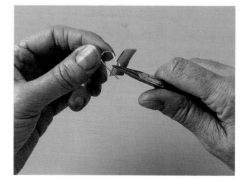

10 Polish both sides of the earrings if desired. Carefully open the ear wires with the jewellery pliers and insert through the drilled holes. Squeeze the wires gently together to close.

This jaunty character is created by photo-etching the design on to a square brooch, leaving a generous frame of silver, then filling the etching with enamel. Follow the colours shown here or choose your own.

Pet Brooch

you will need

silver brooch blank, to fit the template, or 17 gauge/ 1.1mm/0.045in silver sheet

PnP blue acetate film and iron

piercing saw

ring clamp

file

fine emery stick (board)

wooden doming block

wooden doming punch

mallet

nitric acid

brass brush

washing-up liquid (liquid soap)

pestle and mortar

transparent enamels

enamel gum

fine artist's paintbrush or quill

trivet

kiln and firing equipment

diamond-impregnated paper

emery paper

soldering equipment

brooch catch, joint and pin

easy solder

pickle solution

toothbrush

pumice powder

parallel (channel-type) pliers

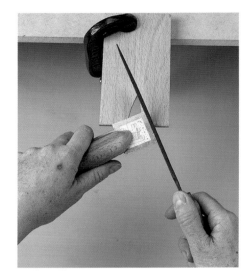

◄ **1** Photocopy the template at the back of the book to produce a high contrast black-and-white design. The design needs to be photo-etched on to the brooch blank or silver sheet (see Enamelling Techniques section) and the template should be copied at the actual size of the finished brooch. If you are using sheet silver, cut out the brooch shape with a piercing saw, place the silver in a clamp and file the edges straight.

2 Polish the edges of the brooch with a fine emery stick to remove any scratch marks left by the file.

3 Place the annealed brooch blank in the doming block. Tap lightly with the punch and mallet until the piece is slightly domed.

4 De-oxidize the silver by placing in nitric acid for a few minutes then rinsing in cold water. Using a brass brush, brush with water and washing-up liquid until shiny. Hold by the edges only.

5 Grind and clean the enamels, then add a drop of enamel gum and water to cover. Apply the wet enamels using a paintbrush or quill. Leave to dry on top of the kiln.

6 Fire in the kiln until the enamel is molten. Leave to cool. Apply further layers of enamel, firing in between each layer, until the cells appear full.

7 Using medium-grade diamond-impregnated paper and water, abrade the enamel until you expose the silver design. Apply more enamel to any shiny areas, then repeat the firing, abrading and rinsing. Refire to glaze the surface.

8 Leave to cool then remove the oxidation from the back of the brooch with emery paper.

9 Place the brooch upside down on a trivet so that only the edges touch. Solder on the brooch catch and joint with easy solder. Leave to cool, then place in pickle solution. Rinse, then clean using a toothbrush and a paste of pumice powder.

10 Polish the brooch if desired. Cut the brooch pin to length and place it in the ball joint. Using parallel pliers, squeeze the joint carefully to hold the pin in place.

Decorate this photo-etched pendant with as many transparent enamel colours as you like, including several shades of green, to evoke the atmosphere of a sunny summer garden in full bloom.

Flower Pendant

you will need

silver pendant blank, to fit the template, or 17 gauge/ 1.1mm/0.045in silver sheet

PnP blue acetate film and iron

piercing saw

ring clamp

file

emery stick (board)

wooden doming block

wooden doming punch

mallet

nitric acid

brass brush

washing-up liquid (liquid soap)

pestle and mortar

transparent enamels

enamel gum

fine artist's paintbrush or quill

trivet

kiln and firing equipment

diamond-impregnated paper

fine-grade emery paper

small piece of silver wire

soldering equipment

easy solder

tweezers

pickle solution

pumice powder or felt

polishing mop (optional)

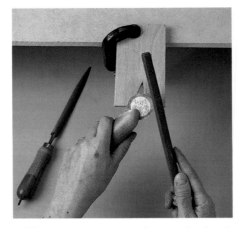

1 Photocopy the template at the back of the book to produce a high contrast black-and-white design. Photo-etch the design on to the silver. Cut out the shape with a piercing saw and file the edges until circular, then smooth with an emery stick.

2 Shape the pendant in a doming block, using a doming punch and mallet. To de-oxidize the silver, place it in nitric acid for a few minutes then rinse with water. Scrub with a brass brush and washing-up liquid solution.

3 Grind and clean the enamels, then add a drop of enamel gum to each and water to cover. Apply the wet enamels using a paintbrush or quill. Take care not to mix the colours. Leave to dry, then fire in the kiln. Leave to cool.

4 Using diamond-impregnated paper and water, abrade the enamel to expose the silver design, then rinse. Apply more enamel to the shiny areas, then repeat. Abrade the enamel and fire again.

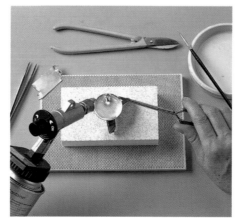

5 Leave to cool, then remove the oxidation from the back of the pendant by rubbing with fine-grade emery paper.

6 Bend the wire into a loop and melt easy solder on to the ends. To attach the loop to the pendant, hold it in tweezers against the back of the pendant and heat the ends until they join. Leave to cool, then pickle and polish the pendant as desired.

A delicately textured surface is created by impressing silver with watercolour paper then applying two enamel colours and flux to create a marbled effect. Small shards of silver foil are fired between the layers.

Shield Earrings

you will need

scissors

rough-textured watercolour paper

20 gauge/0.8mm/0.03in silver sheet

blow torch

general pickle

rolling mill

tracing paper and pencil

double-sided tape

piercing saw

file

drill

burnisher

brass brush

washing-up liquid (liquid soap)

clean cotton cloth

pestle and mortar

transparent enamels: mauve and pale yellow-green

fine artist's paintbrush or quill

borax-based flux (auflux)

trivet

kiln and firing equipment

craft (utility) knife

scraps of fine silver foil

diamond file or carborundum stone

silicon carbide (wet and dry) paper

earring wires

round-nosed (snub-nosed) pliers

2 small domed silver discs

2 frosted beads

2 bead pins

1 Cut a piece of watercolour paper slightly larger than the silver sheet. Anneal the silver and remove the oxidation (see Enamelling Techniques section). Place the silver sheet on top of the paper and run them together through the rolling mill, with the rollers tightly clamped down.

2 Trace the templates at the back of the book to create the main body of both earrings. Attach the tracings to the silver with double-sided tape.

3 Using a piercing saw, cut out the shield shapes. File the edges. Drill small holes in two matching diagonally opposed corners of each shield. ▶

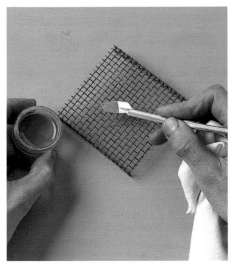

4 Burnish around the sides to raise an edge to contain the enamel. Now scrub the shields with a brass brush and washing-up liquid solution, rinse and dry.

5 Grind and clean the enamels. Using a fine paintbrush or quill, wet-apply the flux and mauve enamel randomly to create a marbled effect. Ensure that they do not run into the drilled holes.

6 Draw off any excess water with a clean cotton cloth. Fire the first layer in the kiln and leave to cool.

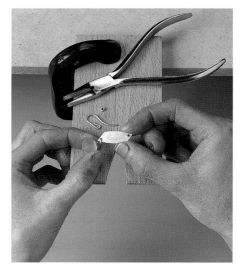

7 Using a craft knife, cut small jagged pieces of silver foil. Moisten the fired enamel with water and apply the pieces of foil in a broken S-shaped line, using a damp paintbrush. Draw off any excess water with a cloth. Wet-apply a spot of flux to one corner of each shield and fire. When the flux has fused, the foil will have adhered to the enamel.

8 When cool, wet-apply the yellow-green enamel over the foil. Apply flux to all other areas and fire. Finally, fire a last layer using flux only.

9 Abrade the fired surface using a diamond file, then rinse and fill in any low spots with more enamel, and re-fire. Remove excess enamel from the edges then finish all sides of the shields with fine-grade silicon carbide paper and rinse. Attach the earring wires to the holes at the top of the earrings and add discs, frosted beads and bead pins to the bottom.

This modern brooch is made in three layers, sandwiching copper between sheets of silver. The design is accentuated by stencil-rolling waves on the silver before enamelling to create a textured effect.

Wave Brooch

you will need

scissors

rough-textured watercolour paper

4 x 2.5cm/1½ x 1in piece of 18 gauge/1mm/0.04in silver sheet

pencil

craft (utility) knife

nitric acid

rolling mill

graver

tracing paper

4 x 6cm/1½ x 2½in piece of 18 gauge/1mm/0.04in copper sheet

piercing saw

scriber

4 x 6cm/1½ x 2½in piece of 20 gauge/0.8mm/0.03in silver sheet

file

drill

4 x 14BA ³/₁₆th cheesehead brass bolts and matching nuts

burnisher

glass fibre brush

washing-up liquid (liquid soap)

pestle and mortar

transparent enamels: turquoise and blue

fine artist's paintbrush or quill

flux

trivet

kiln and firing equipment

carborundum stone or diamond file

silicon carbide (wet and dry) paper

pumice powder

toothbrush

stopping-out varnish

brush cleaner

blowtorch

soldering equipment

hard solder

brooch catch, joint and pin

pickle solution

1 Cut the watercolour paper larger than the piece of 18 gauge silver sheet. Draw stylized wave shapes on the paper and cut out carefully with a craft knife to make a stencil.

2 Anneal the silver sheet. Remove the firestain by placing it in nitric acid until it whitens. Place the paper stencil on top of the sheet. Run them together through the rolling mill, with the rollers tightly clamped down. Emphasize the waves by engraving a few lines around them with a graver.

3 Trace template 1 from the back of the book on to the copper sheet and cut out with a piercing saw. Using a scriber, draw round this shape on to the 20 gauge silver sheet. ▶

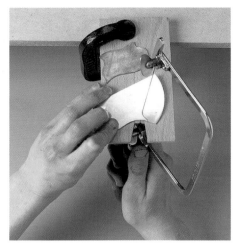

4 Cut out the silver just outside the marked line so that it is slightly larger than the copper shape. Next, trace template 2 on to the rolled, textured silver and cut out. File the edges of all the pieces.

5 Drill a small hole in each corner of the rolled silver to fit the brass screws. Burnish the edges to provide a lip to contain the enamel. Scrub thoroughly with a glass fibre brush and washing-up liquid solution, and then rinse.

6 Grind and clean the enamels. Wet-apply the turquoise enamel, using a paintbrush or quill. Make sure it does not flow into the holes. Fire this layer.

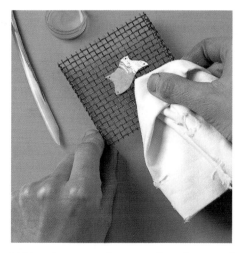

7 For the next three to four layers of enamel, emphasize the wavy lines by shadowing with blue and highlighting them with the flux, applied with a clean, dry cloth.

8 Abrade the fired enamel using a carborundum stone or diamond file. Rinse, fill in low spots and re-fire if necessary. Abrade again, smooth with silicon carbide paper, then scrub with a glass fibre brush under running water. Scrub the back and sides with a paste of pumice powder and water, using a toothbrush.

9 Scrub the copper with pumice powder, then de-grease with a glass fibre brush and washing-up liquid solution. Cover the back and edges with stopping-out varnish and paint a "breezy" border on the front. When the varnish is dry, place the brooch in nitric acid diluted in 3 parts water for about 5 minutes. Rinse, then remove any varnish with brush cleaner. File the edges.

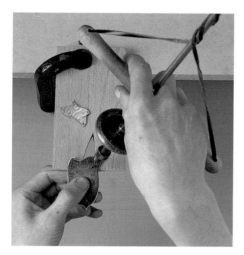 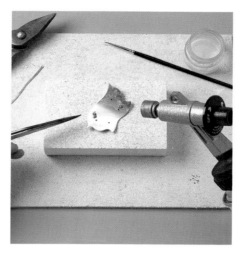 

10 Gently shape the silver and copper backing pieces to match the curve of the enamelled piece. Colour the copper iridescent purple by gently heating it with a blowtorch. Drill holes in both pieces to match the enamelled piece.

11 Solder the brooch fittings on to the backing piece using hard solder. Pickle and rinse. Abrade thoroughly with silicon carbide paper, then with a toothbrush and pumice powder that has been mixed to a paste with water.

12 Clean with a glass fibre brush and washing-up liquid solution. Rivet the brooch pin. Assemble the brooch using brass screws and nuts.

In *cloisonné* work, fine wires are laid down in a pattern to make cells for the enamels. The triangles in this design echo the outline of the silver mounts, and small curls of silver wire add a final flourish.

Cloisonné Earrings

you will need

piercing saw

18 gauge/1mm/0.04in silver sheet

tracing paper and pencil

24 gauge/0.5mm/0.02in silver sheet

double-sided tape

file

fine emery stick (board)

metal snips

16 gauge/1.2mm/0.05in round silver wire

pliers

soldering equipment

hard solder

swage block

wooden doming punch

mallet

silver earring posts and backs

burnisher

glass fibre brush

scissors

28 gauge/0.3mm/0.013in silver *cloisonné* wire

fine artist's paintbrush

enamel gum

trivet

pestle and mortar

transparent enamels: turquoise, light amber, bright blue

quill (optional)

kiln and firing equipment

diamond-impregnated paper

silicon carbide (wet and dry) paper

nail buffer

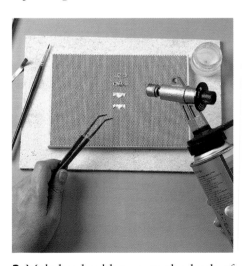

1 Cut two 16 x 22mm/⅝ x ⅞in rectangles from the thicker silver sheet. To create the earring tops, trace template 1 from the back of the book. Attach the tracing to the thinner silver sheet with double-sided tape. Cut out twice, using a piercing saw.

2 File the two cut-out earring tops and smooth the edges with a fine emery stick. Cut two lengths of round silver wire and bend into matching curls with pliers, following the shape of template 2.

3 Melt hard solder on to the back of the earring tops and the straight part of the wire design.

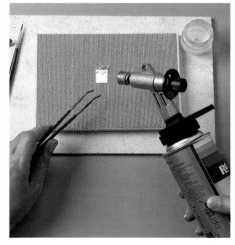

4 Position the earring tops and the wire designs, solder side down, in place on top of the silver rectangles. Flux the metal and rerun the solder with the blowtorch.

5 Place each earring face down in a swage block. Lay a wooden doming punch along its length and tap with a mallet to create a curved shape.

6 Solder the earposts to the earrings with hard solder. Burnish the edges of the earrings to provide a "grip" for the enamel to adhere to. Clean the metal with a glass fibre brush and water.

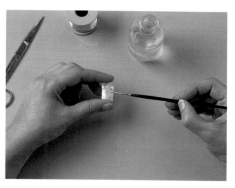

7 Cut the required lengths of *cloisonné* wire and lay on each earring in a geometric pattern, using a fine paintbrush dipped in a little enamel gum. Place on a trivet.

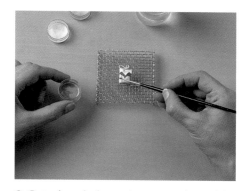

8 Grind and clean the enamels. Add a few drops of enamel gum and water to cover. Using a fine paintbrush or quill, apply the enamel to the cells between the *cloisonné* wires.

9 Allow to dry on top of the kiln, then fire. Apply two more layers of enamel, firing twice more. The enamel should now reach the top of the wire.

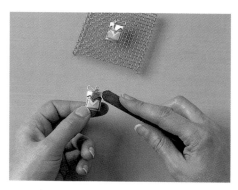

10 Abrade the enamel with diamond-impregnated paper and water to expose any covered *cloisonné* wire. Rinse and re-fire. Smooth the silver with silicon carbide paper and finish with a buffer.

In this brooch, the enamel is applied within *cloisonné* cells and is also enclosed within a wire rectangle, which acts as a frame. The piece shows how this traditional technique perfectly suits a modern design.

Cloisonné Brooch

1 Cut two 5cm/2in lengths of 18 gauge square silver wire. Holding a square needle file at an angle, file a triangular groove 18mm/¾in from one end of each wire, three-quarters of the way through the wire's thickness. Anneal the wires (see Enamelling Techniques section), and bend to right angles at the filed points. Solder the mitre on each wire, using hard solder.

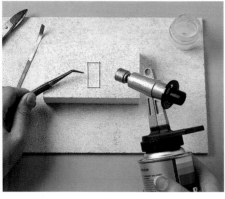

2 File the ends of the two L-shapes at 45° so that they will fit together to make a rectangular frame. Solder together with hard solder.

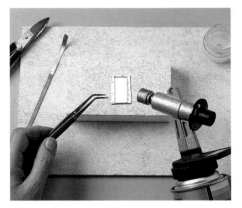

3 Place the wire rectangle on the silver sheet. Lay pieces of hard solder around the outside of the wire frame and solder it to the silver sheet. Cut off the excess silver sheet but do not file the edges until the enamelling is complete.

4 Place the piece in a swage block, with the side to be enamelled face down. Using a wooden punch and mallet, create a curved shape.

▶

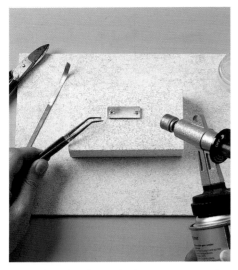

5 Solder the brooch fittings on to the back, using hard solder.

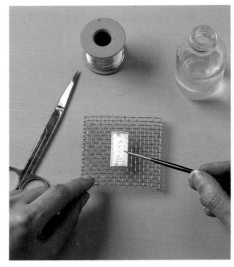

6 Remove firestain and clean the front of the brooch thoroughly with a glass fibre brush and water. Cut the *cloisonné* wire into the required lengths and place on the brooch to make the geometric pattern, using a fine paintbrush dipped in enamel gum.

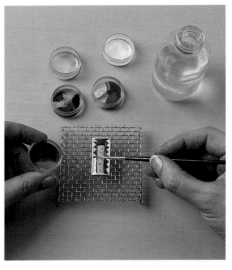

7 Grind and clean the enamels. Add a few drops of enamel gum to each colour, with water to cover. Using a fine artist's paintbrush or a quill, apply the enamel to the cells created by the *cloisonné* wires.

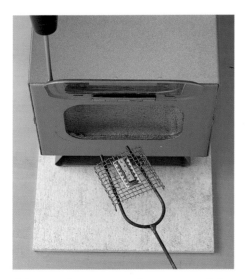

8 Leave the piece to dry on top of the kiln, then fire the enamel. Apply two more layers of enamel, firing each layer. The enamel should now reach the top of the wire.

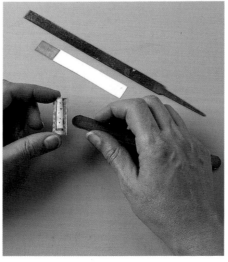

9 Abrade the enamel with diamond-impregnated paper and water until it is even, exposing any *cloisonné* wires that have been covered. Rinse thoroughly with water and a glass fibre brush and re-fire. File the silver around the outer edges of the brooch.

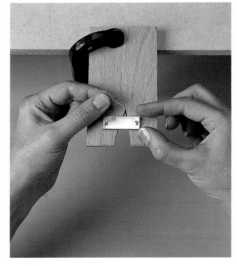

10 Clean and polish the edges of the silver with silicon carbide paper and a nail buffer. Attach the brooch pin using parallel pliers.

The slender elegant shape of this pendant is reminiscent of Art Deco jewellery. A little *cloisonné* detailing has been added within the delicate silver frame, matching its geometric design.

Triangular Pendant

you will need

tracing paper, pencil and ruler

24 gauge/0.5mm/0.02in silver sheet

double-sided tape

piercing saw

drill

file

soldering equipment

hard solder

18 gauge/1mm/0.04in silver sheet

swage block

wooden doming punch

mallet

doming block

silver chain

glass fibre brush

trivet

small, sharp scissors

28 gauge/0.3mm/0.013in fine silver *cloisonné* wire

fine artist's paintbrush

enamel gum

pestle and mortar

transparent enamels: turquoise, light amber, bright blue and grey

quill (optional)

kiln and firing equipment

diamond-impregnated paper

silicon carbide (wet and dry) paper

nail buffer

silver necklace clasp

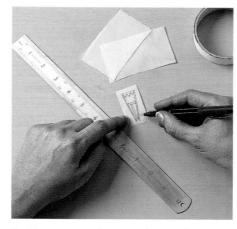

1 Trace template 1 from the back of the book on to tracing paper. Attach the tracing to the 24 gauge silver sheet with double-sided tape.

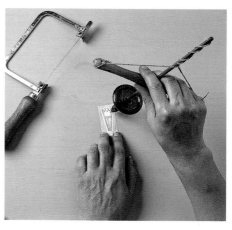

2 Cut out the outer shape with a piercing saw. Drill holes to allow access for the saw blade and cut out the inner parts of the design. File and smooth the inside edges.

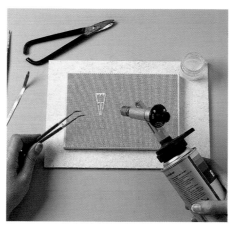

3 Melt some small pieces of hard solder on to the back of the pierced pendant shape.

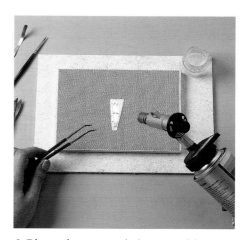

4 Place the pierced shape, solder side down, on the 18 gauge silver sheet. Place hard solder around the outside and solder the pierced shape to the sheet. If any solder runs into the areas that are to be enamelled, it should be removed.

▶

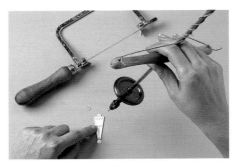

5 Following template 2, saw off the excess silver sheet, leaving a tab at the top for a loop and a circle at the bottom. Do not file the edges. Drill a hole in the centre of both tab and circle.

6 Place the pendant face down in a swage block. Using the doming punch on its side, tap it into a curved shape using a mallet.

7 Cut out a circle of silver sheet fractionally larger than the circle at the bottom of the pendant. Place in a doming block and create a small dome. File the base of the dome flat.

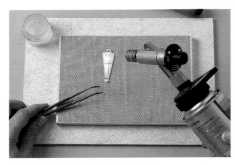

8 Solder the dome on to the circle at the bottom of the pendant with hard solder. Use a piercing saw to make the opening in the tab large enough to take your silver chain. Clean the metal with a glass fibre brush and water. Place on a trivet.

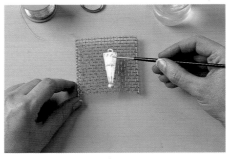

9 Cut the required lengths of *cloisonné* wire and place in the recesses in the pendant to form a geometric pattern, using a fine paintbrush dipped in enamel gum.

10 Grind and clean the enamels. Add a few drops of enamel gum and water to cover. Apply the enamel to the cells, using a fine paintbrush or quill.

11 Leave the enamel to dry on top of the kiln, then fire. Apply two more thin layers of enamel, firing each time.

12 Abrade the enamel with diamond-impregnated paper and water. Clean with a glass fibre brush and water. Re-fire. File the pendant edges. Smooth the silver areas with silicon carbide paper. Finish with a buffer. Thread the chain through the loop. Solder on a clasp and polish.

Adorn patch pockets with these highly original and decorative clips. Galvanized wire has been used here; if you wish, the wire can be sprayed with metallic car paint to change its colour.

Pocket Clips

you will need

wire cutters

18 gauge/1mm/0.04in and 22 gauge/
0.6mm/0.025in galvanized wire

ruler or tape measure

round-nosed (snub-nosed) pliers

half-round jeweller's pliers

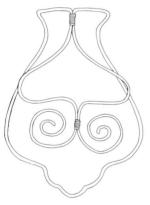

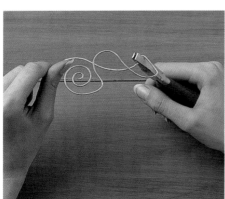

1 Cut a 1m/40in length of 18 gauge galvanized wire. Make a coil at one end with the round-nosed pliers. Bend the wire to make an S-shape, referring to the diagram above. Square off the loop below the coil with half-round pliers.

2 Using half-round pliers, nip in the wire to form one side of the neck, then make a large loop in the wire. From top to bottom the large loop measures 11.5cm/4½in. Make a mirror-image loop and coil on the other side of the large loop, cutting off any excess wire.

3 Fold the structure in half and bend the top of the large loop at both sides to make shoulders. Nip in the bottom of the large loop to make a scallop. Using the 22 gauge wire, bind the coils together and bind the neck for 12mm/½in.

This necklace is great fun to create and is the perfect project to make with children. You could also make matching accessories using clip-on earring backs and headband bases.

Furry Flower Necklace

you will need
round-nosed (snub-nosed) pliers
plain, furry and thick, bumpy
pipe cleaners
coloured paper clips (fasteners)
wired tape
wire cutters

1 Using round-nosed pliers, make small flowers from plain pipe cleaners. Make the centres of the flowers by straightening paper clips and coiling them into spirals. Bend a pipe cleaner into a five-petalled flower and twist the ends together.

2 Coil a plain pipe cleaner and a striped paper clip into a tight, neat spiral to make the centre of the largest flower. Tie a knot in a length of wired tape and thread it neatly through the flower centre so that the knot sits at the front.

3 Bend a thick, bumpy pipe cleaner to form the necklace. Bind the small flowers to the pipe cleaner necklace with the wired tape, tucking in the tape ends behind the flowers. Bind the large flower to a paper clip and clip on to the pipe cleaner necklace.

▲ **4** Form a loop at each end of the pipe cleaner. Attach wired tape to each loop. Coil two paper clips into cones and slide them on to the ends. Bend straightened paper clips into coils and join them together to make two chains. Attach the chains to the ends of the pipe cleaner. Make a "hook-and-eye" fastening from paper clips.

A good way to use up small scraps of tin is to make brooches. These can be simple in construction and made special with some painted decoration. Enamel paints are opaque and look stunning.

Painted Tin Brooch

you will need

30 gauge/0.25mm/0.01in tin sheet

felt-tipped pen

protective gloves

tin snips

bench vice

file

silicon carbide (wet and dry) paper

chinagraph pencil

enamel paints

fine paintbrushes

clear gloss polyurethane varnish

epoxy resin glue

brooch fastener

1 To make the brooch front, draw a circle 5cm/2in in diameter on a piece of tin with a marker pen. Now, making sure first that you are wearing protective gloves, cut out the circle using tin snips.

2 Clamp the tin circle in a bench vice and file the edges. Finish off the edges with damp silicon carbide paper so that they are smooth.

3 Draw a motif on one side of the brooch using a chinagraph pencil. Paint around the outline with enamel paint, then fill in the design. Leave the brooch to dry thoroughly.

4 Paint in the background, then add any features on top of the first coat of paint, using a fine paintbrush and enamel paint. Leave to dry. Seal the surface with two coats of clear gloss polyurethane varnish. Leave to dry thoroughly between coats.

5 Mix some epoxy resin glue and use it to stick a brooch fastener on to the back. Let the glue dry thoroughly before wearing the brooch.

Reproduce the delicate texture of a web in glittering copper and silver wire. The resident spider is resplendent in blue and gold and not at all threatening, especially as she has only six legs and a curly tail!

Spider's Web Brooch

you will need

18 gauge/1mm/0.04in copper wire

ruler

wire cutters

round-nosed (snub-nosed) pliers

22 gauge/0.6mm/0.025in silver wire

self-hardening clay

modelling tool

two small glass beads

brooch pin

epoxy resin glue

turquoise acrylic paint

paintbrush

clear varnish

gold powder

1 Cut four 7.5cm/3in lengths of copper wire. Curl both ends of each piece into a loop using round-nosed pliers.

2 Arrange the pieces to form a star. Wrap the silver wire round the centre. Working outwards in a spiral, twist the silver wire once round each copper wire. Secure and trim.

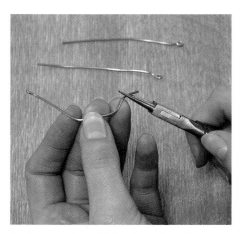

3 Cut six 6cm/2½in lengths of copper wire. Curl one end of each into a tight loop then bend the rest of the length into the shape of the spider's legs.

4 Cut a 7.5cm/3in length of wire and bend it into a spiral for the tail. Roll two balls of self-hardening clay for the body and head.

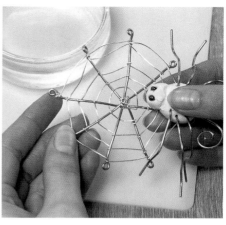

5 Press the two clay balls together, joining securely with the help of the modelling tool. Smooth the surface of the clay with wet fingers or the modelling tool.

6 Insert the looped ends of the wire legs and tail into the spider's body. Press two glass beads into the head to make the eyes.

7 Press the spider's body on to the wire web. Flatten a small piece of clay and attach it to the spider from under-neath the web, using the modelling tool to join it securely. Leave the clay to harden.

8 Glue the brooch pin to the back of the spider, and secure the legs and tail with drops of glue. Paint the body and head turquoise and leave to dry. Apply a coat of varnish to seal the paint. Mix gold powder with a little varnish and apply swiftly with a dry brush to leave some of the turquoise paint showing through.

This jewel box is made from a combination of thin zinc sheet, which has a subtle sheen rather like pewter, and brass shim, which is a fairly soft metal used mostly by sculptors.

Tinware Jewel Box

you will need
protective gloves
tin shears and snips
thin zinc sheet
cigar box
file
pencil, stiff card (stock) and
scissors (for templates)
brass shim
sheet of chipboard (particle board)
hammer and nail
soldering equipment
solder
epoxy resin glue

1 Wearing protective gloves, use tin shears to cut a piece of zinc to cover the lid of the cigar box. The zinc should be slightly larger than the box lid, to allow for a rim to cover the edges of the lid. File the rough edges. Draw a diamond and two different-sized hearts on a sheet of stiff card and cut them out.

2 Place the templates on a piece of brass shim and draw around them – six small hearts, one large heart and two diamonds. Draw some small circles freehand. Draw one small heart on a scrap of zinc. Cut out all the shapes and file the edges smooth. Place the hearts and diamonds on the chipboard and stamp dots around the edge of each using a hammer and nail. Do not stamp the circles or the zinc heart.

◀ **3** Cut four strips of shim to make a border around the zinc lid cover. Place all the pieces on a soldering mat and drop a blob of liquid solder in the centre of the circles, small hearts and diamonds. Cover the zinc heart with solder blobs. Add a line of blobs to each piece of the shim border.

4 Turn down a narrow rim around the zinc panel at 90° to fit over the sides of the lid. Glue all the shapes and the borders to the panel.

5 Cut a strip of zinc the width of the box side and long enough to fit all round it. File the edges smooth. Cut circles of shim, decorate each with a blob of solder and glue in place.

6 Glue the zinc strip around the sides of the box. Glue the zinc panel to the top of the lid. Gently tap the edges of the panel to make them flush with the sides of the lid.

Paper, Card and Wood

As a raw material, paper is both plentiful and adaptable. Turned into durable papier mâché it can be fashioned into beads, sculptural brooches or earrings, and intricate decoupage shapes make a fascinating decorative treatment for even the smallest items. Wood crops up in jewellery design as beautifully turned beads and bangles, or combined with silver or gold in modern pieces, while on a simpler scale it's ideal for making bright, fun badges.

Gorgeous paper is easy to find in specialist stores, but look out for unusual packaging, gift wraps and foils that can be recycled in your jewellery projects, and collect pretty patterns for decoupage designs.

Paper and Card Materials

Cardboard

Double-walled corrugated cardboard makes a firm base for papier mâché, but for small items use stiff, thin card. Single-walled corrugated cardboard is flexible; use it to cover stylish boxes.

Foil

Buy gold, silver or coloured foil from craft stores or use sweet (candy) papers.

Gift wrap

Printed wrapping paper is a good source of decoupage images.

Glue

PVA (white) glue is ideal for sticking paper and card. It can also be diluted and used to soak newspaper for papier mâché as an alternative to wallpaper paste. Use strong epoxy resin glue to attach jewellery findings to your finished pieces.

Newspaper

Tear newspaper into thin strips and soak in wallpaper paste or dilute PVA (white) glue to make papier mâché.

Paints

Gouache and acrylic paints dry quickly and are easy to use. For brilliant, glossy colour and sparkling metallic effects, use enamel paint.

Papier mâché pulp

You can make papier mâché pulp easily yourself (see Paper and Card Techniques) or buy it ready-made from craft suppliers. It is strengthened with a filler such as plaster of Paris and is ideal for building up sculpted shapes that can then be covered with strips of paper ready for decorating.

Primer

Painting papier mâché shapes with one or two coats of white acrylic primer will provide a good surface for decoration.

Sanding sealer/shellac

This toffee-coloured, spirit-based lacquer can be used to seal and strengthen paper and card and to give an antique look to painted finishes.

Varnish

Several coats of glossy acrylic or oil-based varnish protect a painted surface and make colours glow. Crackle varnish is a two-part treatment that gives an antique look and is especially effective with decoupage designs.

The equipment needed for working with paper and card is minimal, and you will probably already have nearly everything you need. Some woodworking tools are useful when shaping papier mâché.

Paper and Card Equipment

Abrasive paper
Hard papier mâché can be smoothed by rubbing it down with medium- and fine-grade abrasive paper.

Blender
If you want to make your own papier mâché pulp, whizzing the soaked and boiled paper in a blender produces a smooth texture very easily.

Bowl
Use an old mixing bowl to dilute PVA (white) glue or mix wallpaper paste for papier mâché.

Craft (utility) knife
Replace the blade of a craft knife or scalpel often as paper and card will quickly blunt it. Always use a cutting mat to protect the work surface.

Cutting mat
A self-healing cutting mat is an ideal cutting surface.

Paintbrushes
A selection of artist's brushes is useful for applying glue and smoothing down layers of papier mâché as well as for painting. To paint decorative lines use a coachliner (liner) brush: this has long hairs of uniform length and is designed to hold a lot of paint so that you don't have to keep lifting the brush to reload it.

Pencil and ruler
For tracing templates and marking out designs. Use a metal ruler with a craft knife to cut straight lines.

Scissors
Use general household scissors for cutting paper and card. Don't use dressmaking shears as they will quickly be blunted. A pair of small, sharp-pointed scissors is essential for cutting out decoupage images accurately.

Sponge
A natural sponge can be used to create paint effects, to stick down decoupage motifs and wipe off excess paste, and to apply glazes.

Many different decorative techniques are possible using paper and card: just experiment with the materials that inspire you. Papier mâché and papier mâché pulp are both excellent for sculpting items of jewellery.

Paper and Card Techniques

Papier Mâché   Newspaper is most commonly used for papier mâché and is very pliable and strong. For very delicate items you could try using tissue paper, though it is tricky to handle when wet.

1 Tear the newspaper into strips about 2cm/¾in wide. Tearing with the grain makes it easy to produce regular strips. Dilute PVA (white) glue with water to the consistency of single (light) cream or use fungicide-free wallpaper paste.

2 Use a paintbrush to coat each strip of paper in the glue or paste and press it on to a cardboard base, or into a mould. Use the brush to smooth the paper down and expel any air bubbles.

3 When you have built up the shape, leave to dry completely. Sand the surface smooth if necessary and hide the newsprint with two coats of white acrylic primer before decorating.

Making Papier Mâché Pulp

Prepared pulp can be bought but it's easy to make. You will need:

5 sheets newspaper

60ml/4 tbsp PVA (white) glue

10ml/2 tsp plaster of Paris

10ml/2 tsp linseed oil

Tear the paper into small squares, place in an old saucepan with water to cover and simmer for 30 minutes. Pour into a blender and blend to a pulp. Add the other ingredients and stir vigorously. Pulp can be stored for some weeks in a plastic box.

Working with Papier Mâché Pulp

You can use paper pulp very effectively to build up sculpted forms, simply pushing it into shape with your fingers. Allow plenty of time for the pulp to dry out thoroughly before completing the project.

1 To make a three-dimensional piece, build up the papier mâché pulp on a base such as a cardboard shape. Leave to dry out thoroughly.

2 When the pulp shape is dry and hard, cover it completely with two layers of papier mâché and leave to dry before decorating.

Decoupage

Though most often associated with furniture and decorative household items, paper cutouts can be used to enhance many different objects, large or small. Glass, metal, wood and china are all suitable surfaces.

Surface Preparation

Whatever you are decorating, it is vital to have an absolutely smooth surface to achieve a "painted on" look.

1 Sand wood smooth with medium- then fine-grade abrasive paper. Prime and sand again, then apply two coats of paint. If you want to leave the wood grain visible, seal the surface with shellac before decorating.

2 Metal should be scrubbed and coated with red oxide primer to provide a key for paint. If you are using a light-coloured paint, apply one or two coats of white acrylic primer.

Painting Edges

On items such as boxes, painted edges can enhance a decoupage design. Choose a colour that contrasts with the base colour and goes well with the cutout designs. It's advisable to paint lines before adding cutouts, in case of mistakes.

Load a coachliner (liner) brush with acrylic paint diluted with a little water. Holding the brush like a pen, and using the edge of your hand as a support, drag the brush towards you. Use your little finger against the edge to keep your hand steady. Lift the brush gradually when you get near the end of the line so that it doesn't drag over the edge. If you need to reload the brush before reaching the end, overlap the lines a little to ensure continuity.

Tinting Prints

Black and white prints are easily enhanced with delicate colour.

Subtle effects can be achieved using coloured pencils. Start with the lighter areas, working with gentle strokes in one direction. Build up the colour gradually, blending it carefully. Seal tinted prints with sanding sealer and leave to dry before cutting out.

Cutting Out Motifs

Whether you prefer to use a pair of scissors or a craft (utility) knife, the basic principles remain the same. Always use a cutting mat with a craft knife.

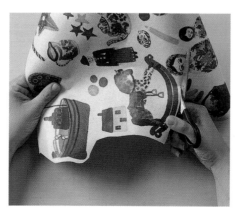

1 Cut the excess paper from around the outer edge of the motif using a large pair of scissors.

2 Cut away any background areas within the design, piercing a hole in the centre of the area then cutting outwards to the edge. Cut around the outside edge without leaving any trace of background: it is better to cut slightly inside the edge of the motif.

Gluing Motifs

PVA (white) glue is suitable for decoupage on most surfaces. Dilute the glue with a little water to make it spreadable. A glue stick can be used for very small designs, especially on paper or card (stock).

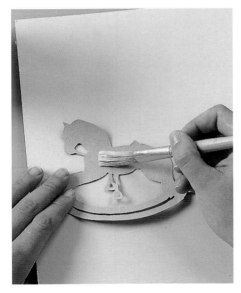 

1 Use an artist's brush to paint glue over the back of the motif, thinly covering the entire surface right up to the edges. Alternatively, if the motif has a very intricate design and might be damaged by the brush, you can paint the glue on the base surface, wiping away any excess while still wet after positioning the motif.

2 Lay the cutout gently on the surface. When you are satisfied with its position, press it down gently with your fingers or a barely moistened sponge, starting at the centre and smoothing outwards. When you are working on a small piece you can hold the work up to the light to highlight any air bubbles or areas that have not adhered properly.

3 Lift any edges that have been missed and dab on some more glue if necessary. Leave for a few minutes then gently wipe away excess glue using a damp sponge and leave to dry.

Varnishing

Careful varnishing protects the decoupage, adds depth to the design and completes the illusion that it is a painted surface. Build the varnish up in a series of thin coats, sanding gently between each. Matt (flat) acrylic varnish is easy to apply and dries quickly, but you may like to finish with a few coats of durable oil-based varnish to protect the surface. For an aged effect brush a little thinned raw umber paint over the varnished surface, leave a few minutes, then wipe off with a cloth.

◀ A crackle finish gives an antique look. It can be applied over varnish and consists of two layers: a slow-drying base and a quick-drying top coat that cracks as the first layer dries out. Apply the second coat when the first feels dry but slightly tacky. If no cracks appear as it dries the process can be speeded up by playing a cool hairdryer over the surface. Rub a little artist's oil paint into the cracks to emphasize them: raw umber is the colour most commonly used. Finish with two coats of oil-based varnish.

Wood is an infinitely adaptable material to work with. Chunky wooden beads and bangles make the most of its natural grain and colours, but it's also an ideal base for paint and other applied decorations.

Woodworking Materials and Equipment

Abrasive paper

Small abrasive particles, glued to backing paper, are graded according to their size: the finer the grit, the smoother the finish.

Bradawl/Awl

The sharp point can be twisted into wood without splitting the grain and is used for scribing and piercing guide holes for drilling.

Drill

A hand drill can be used for quickly making small holes in wood to take jewellery fixings. An electric mini-drill is a convenient alternative.

Glue

PVA (white) glue dries clear and is ideal for joining pieces of wood, though for small projects a hot glue gun is fast and convenient. Use strong epoxy resin glue to attach jewellery findings securely.

Paintbrushes

You could use artist's brushes for most jobs, but ideally use a fine decorating brush for primers and undercoats and artist's brushes to decorate small pieces. Varnishing brushes have long, flat bristles to minimize brush marks.

Paints

Acrylic paints are ideal for painting wood. Start with a coat or two of white acrylic primer to give a smooth, clean surface so that the colours of your design look clear and bright.

Plywood

Birch-faced plywood is smooth and strong and because of its construction will not warp or split. Thin plywood suitable for small projects such as badges is available in small sheets from model and craft suppliers.

Saws

Frame saws are designed for intricate cutting. They work on the pull stroke so blades should always be fitted with the points facing towards the handle.
Coping saw – This is fine for small projects and can be fitted with a range of disposable blades.
Fretsaw – This cuts more deeply than the coping saw as it has a larger frame.

Square

A try square is essential for accurate marking out of right angles.

Varnish

Both acrylic and oil-based varnishes are available in a range of finishes from matt to high gloss. Several thin coats of gloss varnish will make bright paint colours glow like enamels.

Fine details are all-important when you are working on a small scale. Accurate marking out and cutting, meticulous smoothing of the wood, and painstaking surface finishes are the keys to success.

Woodworking Techniques

Transferring Designs

◄ **1** Draw or trace the design and scale it up if necessary by copying it on graph paper of a larger scale or using the enlarging facility on a photocopier. Cut out an accurate template from thin card (stock) and draw around it on the wood using a sharp pencil. For square or rectangular items such as boxes it's essential to check all right angles with a try square when marking out the component parts.

2 Use compasses to draw circles directly on wood. For a motif such as a sun, adjust the compasses and draw an inner circle as a guide for drawing the rays.

Using a Frame Saw

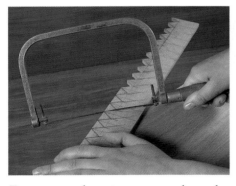

Fret saws and coping saws work on the pull stroke for accurate control. The frame allows the blade to be swivelled for cutting curves. The wood should be clamped so that there is clearance underneath all the lines of the design to move the saw.

If you are cutting out a pierced design, use a hand drill to make a starter hole in each inner section. The removable blade of the saw can then be fed through and re-attached. Saw carefully to the edge of the marked shape and then follow the outline.

Smoothing Surfaces

Many different materials are used to make abrasive papers, generally known as sandpapers. Glasspaper, in medium and fine grades, is suitable for smoothing wood before decorating. Silicon carbide paper is more hard-wearing. Dark grey silicon paper, known as "wet and dry" paper, needs lubricating with water and can be used for fine smoothing of painted and varnished finishes on wood.

Sand all sawn edges until they feel smooth and splinter-free to the touch. Wrap a square of abrasive paper around a wooden or cork sanding block for best results on flat surfaces. Make sure the block is free of defects to avoid scoring the surface of the wood.

For smoothing curved areas wrap a small piece of abrasive paper around your finger, or fold it abrasive side out to get into tight angles.

This glittering star-shaped brooch in papier mâché makes an ideal birthday badge if you decorate it with the appropriate sign of the zodiac: the colourful design used here represents Cancer the Crab.

Star-sign Brooch

you will need

scrap paper, pencil and scissors (for template)

corrugated cardboard

craft (utility) knife

self-healing cutting mat

newspaper

PVA (white) glue

artist's brushes

white acrylic primer

gouache paints: light blue, yellow, red

gloss acrylic varnish

gold enamel paint

brooch back

epoxy resin glue

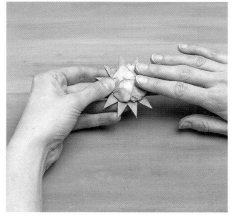

1 Draw a star shape on to scrap paper, cut it out and draw around this shape on to the corrugated cardboard. Now cut out the cardboard star shape. Soak some newspaper in diluted PVA glue, scrunch it up and mound it in the centre of the star.

2 Cover the whole brooch in several layers of newspaper strips soaked in PVA glue. Allow to dry.

3 Give the brooch a coat of PVA glue, then one of white acrylic primer. Allow to dry, paint on the design and then the clear gloss varnish.

4 Add gold enamel paint details. Finally, fix a brooch back in place using epoxy resin glue.

Use papier mâché to create an unusual summery bracelet, decorated with slices of different citrus fruits. Glints of gold picking out the details on the fruit echo the sparkling gold foil lining inside.

Fruity Bracelet

you will need
tracing paper, pencil, paper or card
(stock) (for template)
scissors
thin cardboard
masking tape
large hook and eye
newspaper
PVA (white) glue
strong clear glue
artist's brushes
gold foil (from a chocolate wrapper)
white acrylic primer
acrylic paints: yellow, red,
orange and gold
gloss acrylic varnish

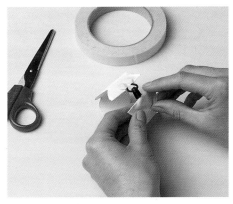

1 Copy the template at the back of the book, enlarging it to fit your wrist, to make a paper or card template. Use this template to cut the shape out of thin cardboard. Tape a large hook to one end of the cardboard bracelet and a matching eye to the other.

2 Tear newspaper into strips and soak in diluted PVA glue. Cover the cardboard with several layers of papier mâché, covering all the edges neatly. Leave to dry. Use strong, clear glue to stick a sheet of gold foil to the inside of the bracelet. Trim the edges.

3 Prime the outside of the bracelet with a coat of white acrylic primer to smooth the surface. Decorate with slices of citrus fruit using acrylic paints. Add touches of gold paint around the edges, pips and dimples.

4 When the paint is dry, protect with several coats of gloss acrylic varnish.

This lavishly decorated box is a stylish way to present a gift of jewellery. You can use paper ribbon both to cover the box and to tie the chunky bow on top, which is trimmed with a posy of fabric flowers.

Presentation Box

you will need

scissors

paper ribbon

oval cardboard box with lid

PVA (white) glue

paintbrush

corrugated cardboard

pencil

selection of fabric flowers

1 Cut a piece of paper ribbon long enough to fit around the rim of the box lid, allowing a small overlap. Unfurl, brush with glue and stick in place. Fold and glue the excess ribbon under and above the rim.

2 Place the lid on the corrugated cardboard with the corrugations running straight from end to end. Draw around the edge and cut out the shape. Glue on to the lid to cover the surplus ribbon.

3 Cut two lengths of ribbon each measuring three times the width of the lid. Unfurl, and glue one end of each piece to the lid, tucking the ends under the rim. Tie the other ends together in a large bow. Trim.

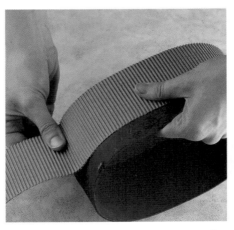

4 Put the lid on the box. Measure the distance from the bottom of the box to the lower edge of the lid. Cut a strip of corrugated cardboard to fit this width, long enough to wrap around the box. Glue in place.

5 Cut the fabric flowers and leaves from their wire stalks. Glue on to the box, so that they give the effect of a sheaf of flowers lying on the lid underneath the bow.

Beads made from paper were traditionally used to make bead curtains, but this old technique can also transform good-quality printed paper into colourful abstract designs for beautiful necklaces and bracelets.

Rolled-paper Beads

you will need
ruler
pencil
gift wrap
scissors
glue stick or PVA (white) glue
gloss acrylic varnish
varnish brush
thin elastic

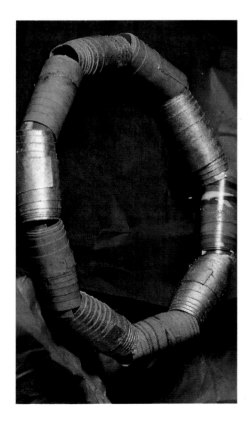

1 Draw a series of 2.5cm/1in-wide strips on the back of a sheet of gift wrap. Now make a mark halfway along one short edge of each strip. Draw lines from the two opposite corners to the marked point, in such a way that you are dividing the strip into long, thin triangles.

2 Cut along the lines on each strip. The central triangle will make a symmetrical bead. Use the right-angled triangles if you want to make conical beads, such as for earrings or the ends of a necklace.

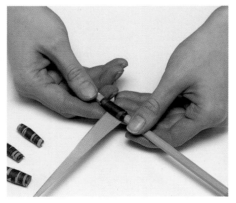

3 Starting at the base of the triangle, roll each strip of paper tightly around a pencil. Make sure the end is correctly aligned with the pencil when you begin so that the bead is symmetrical. After the first turn, apply glue to the wrong side of the paper.

4 Put a little extra glue on the end of the paper triangle and press it down firmly. Leave the bead on the pencil until the glue is dry. The beads can be strengthened and protected with a few coats of acrylic varnish before they are threaded on thin elastic.

This exotic piece of jewellery is made from papier mâché pulp, hand-painted in gorgeous colours and then decorated with artificial gemstones and glass tear-drops.

Winged Cupid Brooch

you will need

tracing paper

pencil

thin card (stock)

craft (utility) knife

cutting mat

papier mâché pulp

newspaper

PVA (white) glue

white acrylic primer

artist's brushes

flat-backed glass gems

epoxy resin glue

dressmaker's pin

eye-hook pins

gouache paints

matt (flat) acrylic varnish

gold enamel paint

small glass tear-drop beads

small jump-rings

round-nosed (snub-nosed) pliers

brooch back

1 Trace the template from the back of the book, transfer it to card and cut out all of the sections. Cover the card pieces with papier mâché pulp and apply several layers of newspaper strips soaked in PVA glue. Allow to dry completely.

2 Paint with a coat of PVA glue, then with white primer. Glue on the glass gems using epoxy resin glue. Make holes using a pin and insert the eye-hook pins, securing them with epoxy resin glue.

3 Paint on the design with gouache paints. When dry, coat with matt varnish. Leave to dry again, then add gold enamel details.

4 Assemble all the brooch pieces and tear-drop beads, joining them with jump-rings (using the pliers). Glue the brooch back into position.

This little trinket box with its pretty posy of roses is ideal for small pieces of jewellery and adds a feminine touch to a dressing-table. Crackle varnish gives the rose design a lovely antique look.

Decoupage Roses Box

you will need

small wooden box with lid
screwdriver
small paintbrush
white acrylic primer
fine-grade abrasive paper
cream emulsion (latex) paint
artist's acrylic paints in raw umber
and gold
coachliner (liner) brush
acrylic varnish
printed rose motifs
small sharp-pointed scissors
metal ruler
pencil
PVA (white) glue
craft (utility) knife
crackle varnish
hairdryer
raw umber oil paint
kitchen paper
white spirit (paint thinner)
oil-based varnish

1 Remove the box lid. Paint the box with a coat of acrylic primer and leave to dry. Lightly sand the surface, then follow with two coats of cream emulsion paint.

2 Now prepare some antique-effect gold paint by mixing a little raw umber and artist's gold acrylic paint with just a touch of water. Then, very carefully lay your coachliner brush in the gold paint and ensure that the brush is thoroughly covered.

▲ 3 Place the brush on one edge of the box rim and drag it along to the end. Now paint all of the edges on the base and lid of your box with gold paint, as described in step 2. Leave until completely dry. Follow with an even coat of acrylic varnish, used to protect the base colour.

▲ 4 With small sharp-pointed scissors, cut out the rose-heads, making sure that you choose colours that complement each other. Use different designs for the front and sides.

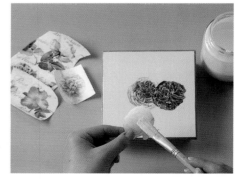

▲ 5 Measure the width and length of the box lid with a ruler to find the centre. Mark this point with a pencil. Dilute some PVA glue with a little water and brush it on to the back of the first rose. Stick it in the centre of the box lid, then add the rest, one at a time, around the central rose until you have a circle.

6 Fit the lid on to the base but don't screw the hinges back on. Apply the designs to the back, front and sides, sticking your motifs over the join (seam) of the lid and base. Leave the box to dry.

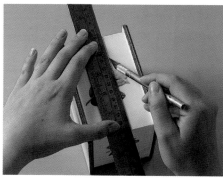

◄ **7** Place a metal ruler along the edge of the join over which you have stuck the motif and draw a very sharp craft knife along the join, making sure that you cut really cleanly through the paper. Repeat on the other two sides.

▶

8 Seal the the surface by brushing on 5–10 coats of acrylic varnish. Allow each coat to dry throughly before applying the next.

9 Following the manufacturer's instructions, brush on the first stage of the crackle varnish and leave until slightly tacky to the touch (about 1–2 hours, although this can vary).

10 Brush on the second stage of the crackle varnish, making sure that you have covered all areas. Leave to dry naturally for about 1–2 hours.

11 If no cracks have appeared, use a hairdryer on its lowest setting and move it over the surface until the cracks begin to appear.

12 Put a tiny amount of raw umber oil paint on to kitchen paper moistened with white spirit and wipe over all surfaces of the box.

13 Take a clean sheet of kitchen paper and wipe off the excess, leaving the paint only in the cracks. Leave to dry overnight. Varnish with two coats of oil-based varnish. Screw the lid and base of the box back together.

Wear one of these jolly badges as a colourful and bold brooch on a plain coat or sweater. Simple to make, these badges are bound to lift your spirits in the morning.

Sun and Moon Badges

you will need

tracing paper, pencil, card (stock) and scissors (for templates)

5mm/¼in birch plywood sheet

coping saw or fretsaw

medium- and fine-grade abrasive paper

white acrylic primer

artist's brushes

acrylic paints: yellow, red and blue

gloss acrylic varnish

epoxy resin or hot glue

2 brooch backs

1 Make card templates (size as wished) from those at the back of the book, and draw round them on to the wood. Cut out the shapes with the saw and sand the edges smooth.

2 Paint both sides and all the edges of the shapes with white acrylic primer. When the paint is dry, sand the surfaces lightly until smooth.

3 Paint the fronts of the sun and moon with acrylic paint and add the features and other details. When the paint is dry, add a coat of varnish and leave to dry. Put a thick line of glue on the back of each badge and press the brooch back firmly into the glue.

The sunflower is an enduringly popular image and an effective stylized motif. Simply painted in warm yellows, this cheerful little badge makes a bright decoration for a plain sweater or a denim jacket.

Sunflower Badge

you will need

5mm/¼in birch plywood sheet

pencil

pair of compasses

coping saw or fretsaw

medium- and fine-grade abrasive paper

PVA (white) glue

white acrylic primer

artist's brushes

acrylic paints: yellow, red, chocolate-brown and gold

gloss acrylic varnish

brooch back

epoxy resin glue

1 Draw a circle for the flower-centre on the plywood with the compasses. Draw the petals freehand around the centre. Draw another circle the same size as the centre. Cut out these two shapes with a saw.

2 Sand any rough edges on the flower and sand the edge of the circle to a curve. Glue the circle to the centre of the flower shape using PVA glue. Paint with white primer and allow to dry. Sand lightly.

◄ **3** Paint in the flower details with the acrylic paints. Mix yellow and red to make a golden-yellow for the petals. Paint the centre brown. When dry, add gold dots to the centre. Apply a coat of gloss varnish. Attach the brooch back using epoxy resin glue.

This jolly little shooting star can be decorated as fancifully as you like in brilliant contrasting colours. Use pearlized paint for its tail and add several coats of glossy varnish to make the colours glow.

Shooting Star Badge

you will need

tracing paper

pencil

4mm/⅙in birch plywood sheet

coping saw or fretsaw

medium- and fine-grade abrasive paper

white acrylic primer

artist's brushes

acrylic paints

water-based pearlized paints

gloss acrylic varnish

brooch back

epoxy resin glue

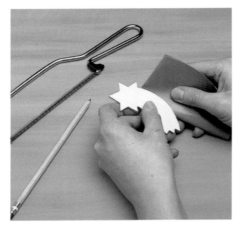

1 Trace the template at the back of the book and transfer to the plywood. Cut out. Sand all the edges.

2 Paint with a coat of white acrylic primer. When dry, sand lightly and mark the remaining points of the star.

3 Paint on the badge's design in acrylic paints, using pearlized paint for the tail. Protect with several coats of gloss varnish.

4 Glue the brooch back on to the badge using epoxy resin glue.

This attractive little box is easy to construct, but the delicate painting and the raised crab design make it unusual and eye-catching. The lid is decorated with a wavy pattern inspired by the crab's watery home.

Crab Jewel Box

you will need

coping saw or fret saw

40cm/16in pine slat, 3cm x 8mm/
1¼ x ⅜in

4mm/⅙in birch plywood sheet

ruler

tracing paper, pencil, card (stock) and scissors (for template)

abrasive paper

wood glue

masking tape

artist's brushes

white acrylic primer

acrylic paints: blue, gold and red

matt (flat) acrylic varnish

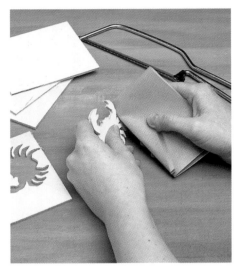

1 Cut the pine slat into four 10cm/4in lengths. From the plywood cut two rectangles measuring 8 x 10cm/3¼ x 4in for the base and lid insert, and one measuring 11.5 x 10cm/4½ x 4in for the lid. Enlarge the crab template at the back of the book, transfer it to the plywood and cut it out. Remove rough edges with abrasive paper.

2 Assemble the sides of the box and stick with wood glue. Hold the sides in place with masking tape until the glue is completely dry. Glue in the base. Glue the lid insert centrally on to the lid. Sand again to smooth any rough edges.

◀ **3** Paint the box and crab with a coat of white acrylic primer. Sand lightly when dry. Paint the box and the lid in blue, thinned with water and applied with wavy brushstrokes. Paint on the border pattern and stars. Paint the crab in red and pick out details in blue and gold. Finish off with a coat of varnish. When dry, glue the crab firmly on to the lid of the box.

Clay, Mosaics and Glass

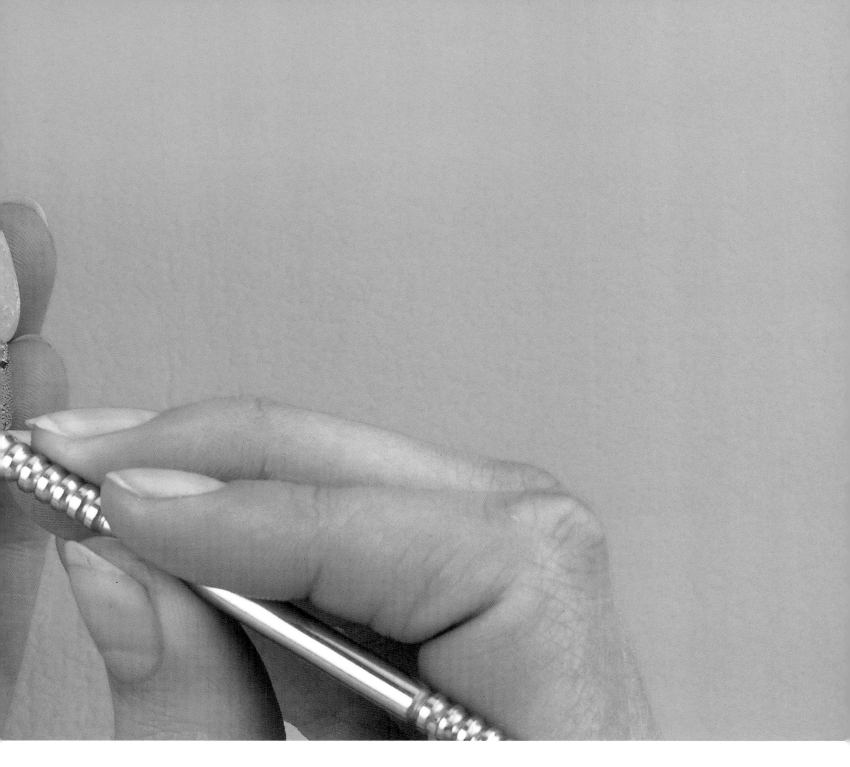

Modelling clay is an ideal medium for intricate ornaments such as buttons, earrings and beads. You can roll it, coil it and shape it in fancy moulds, and a host of different surface textures are possible. Using polymer clay, which is made in a huge range of colours and special effects, you can even achieve complex millefiori designs and sophisticated metallic finishes. The chapter ends with some sparkling ideas for trinket boxes in mosaic and glass.

Choose from self-hardening modelling clay – which does not require firing and can be painted, varnished or gilded once dry – or colourful polymer clay, which is hardened by baking in a domestic oven.

Claywork Materials

Bronze powder

This is a fine metallic powder that is available in gold, silver, copper and other colours. Mix the powder with varnish and brush on to produce a gilded effect.

Button backs

Self-cover buttons are useful for making clay buttons.

Clay hardeners

Powdered hardeners can be mixed into modelling clay before the clay is shaped and they harden the clay throughout. Liquid hardeners seal and harden the outside only.

Glass gemstones and beads

Beads for embedding in clay should be flat-backed. If beads are mounted in clay that is to be fired, they must be made of glass.

Glue

PVA (white) glue will be suitable for holding hardened clay, but epoxy resin is stronger. Diluted PVA glue is commonly used as a sealant on modelling clay.

Jewellery wire

Use this fine wire to connect clay pieces for jewellery items such as earrings and necklaces.

Metallic leaf

Both modelling clay and polymer clay can be gilded. Dutch metal leaf, in gold, silver, copper and aluminium, is easier to apply than real gold.

Modelling clay

Clay comes in many brands and qualities. Air-dried modelling clay needs no firing, but you can strengthen some brands by baking or adding hardeners. Follow manufacturer's instructions.

Paint

Artist's acrylics or acrylic craft paints are suitable for decorating modelling clay and can also be applied to polymer clay. Many effects are possible with special paints: metallic or pearlized colour, verdigris and crackle glaze.

Polymer clay

Actually a plastic (polyvinyl chloride), polymer clay is clean to work with, does not shrink and needs only a low-temperature firing. Already coloured, it needs no further decoration except for special effects such as gilding. It is available in many colours, plus translucent and glow-in-the-dark effects.

Varnish

Gloss or matt (flat) varnish specially formulated for polymer clay is available. Acrylic spray varnish is convenient for small projects.

The most important tools required for working with modelling and polymer clay are your hands. Many ordinary items such as knitting needles, dough cutters and knives can be used for shaping clay.

Claywork Equipment

Airtight boxes and bags

Polymer clay goes crumbly if exposed to heat and daylight. Wrap it in greaseproof paper before storing it in a box. Spare modelling clay should be kept soft inside a plastic bag – moisten the inside of the bag if necessary.

Baking parchment

A sheet of parchment taped to the work surface gives a smooth surface for modelling. Finished models can also be placed on it for baking.

Brayer

This small roller is used to smooth clay and for applying metal leaf.

Knives

A very sharp slim-bladed craft (utility) knife is needed when working with small pieces of polymer clay, and a surgical tissue blade can cut very thin slices without distorting patterns.

Mirror

Placed behind the work, a mirror helps you to see all round the clay for accurate cutting and shaping.

Modelling tools

Many different shapes are available for shaping and smoothing clay. Dental probes make excellent precision tools for modelling. Cocktail sticks and toothpicks are often useful.

Oven

Polymer clay can be hardened in a domestic oven. Accurate temperature control is important as clay burns easily but is fragile if undercooked.

Paintbrushes

Artist's brushes are needed for applying paints and bronze powders.

Pasta machine

Use this to roll out polymer clay to precise, even thicknesses and to mix colours together. Keep a machine solely for use with clay, and wipe it clean when changing colours.

Pastry cutters and moulds

Cake decorating suppliers are a good source of tools. A wheeled pastry cutter can be used to make zigzag edges. Skewers are useful for shaping clay and for holding clay beads during baking.

Plexiglass

This rigid clear plastic makes a smooth modelling surface and a small sheet is used to roll polymer clay canes to reduce their diameter uniformly.

Rolling pin

A vinyl or straight-sided glass roller is best for rolling out clay.

As polymer clay picks up any dirt and dust around, your hands must be scrupulously clean and you should wash them each time you change from one colour to another, to avoid discolouring the clay.

Polymer Clay Techniques

Preparing Polymer Clay

The clay must be kneaded before it is worked. As it is responsive to temperature the warmth of your hands contributes to the conditioning process. Work small amounts, about one-eighth of a block, at a time. Roll the clay into a sausage between your palms then bend it over and roll again, until it is soft and pliable. Try to avoid trapping air bubbles. A pasta machine can be used to knead the clay and to mix colours.

Mixing Colours

Although polymer clay is available in many colours, you can mix more subtle shades yourself. When mixing dark and light colours add tiny bits of the dark clay to the lighter colour to avoid overpowering it.

Rolling out

A pasta machine can be used to produce sheets of uniform thickness, or you can roll the clay out by hand on a smooth clean surface.

To achieve an even thickness throughout the sheet, place two equal-sized pieces of wood, metal or plastic, matching the required depth, on either side of the clay.

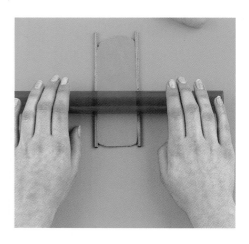

1 Twist together two or more sausages of clay in different colours.

Making Beads

A basic round bead is made by simply rolling a ball of clay between the palms of your hands. You may find that it is quite difficult to make a hole in soft clay without distorting it, so an effective alternative method is to drill the hole after the clay has been baked.

2 Roll the twisted clay into a smooth log then twist, stretch and double over, excluding any air. The clay can be used in this marbled state. Continue to work it to blend colours completely.

1 Make a hole in an unbaked bead using a drilling action with a tapered tool such as a darning needle. When it emerges, remove it and push it through from the other side to neaten the hole.

2 To prevent beads distorting during baking, support them on skewers or wire, suspended across a baking tray.

Clay Cane Work

Clay sheets of different colours can be stacked or rolled together with gentle pressure and then sliced to create a variety of patterns. Derived from glassworking techniques, cane work creates a roll with a design running along its length from which slices can be cut.

Jelly Roll

This technique creates a log that is sliced to create a simple spiral pattern.

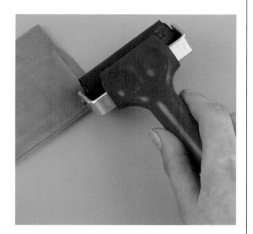

1 Stack two or three sheets of polymer clay together and trim the edges to form a rectangle. Roll a brayer over one of the shorter edges to taper it.

2 Starting at the tapered end, roll up the layers tightly and evenly. Roll the cane to smooth the seam and trim each end flat.

Picture Cane

Simple images can be made into canes. Choose a strong shape and use boldly contrasting colours so that the picture stays clear when the size is reduced.

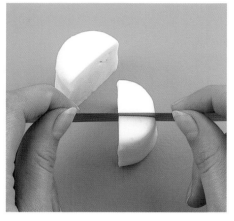

1 Roll a cane of white polymer clay about 3.5cm/1½in in diameter. Cut it in half lengthways using a tissue blade. Curve one half to make the duck's body and cut the other half in two to make two quarters.

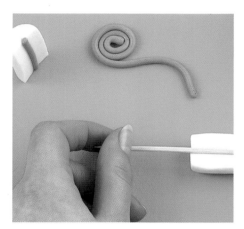

2 Roll one quarter into a round and cut in half again. Make a groove down the middle of one flat side and run a thin sausage of blue clay down it. Groove the other half and sandwich together to make the head and eye.

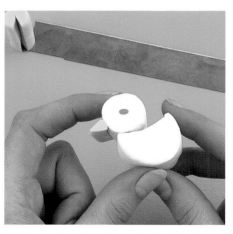

3 Place the head on the body. Cut a triangular wedge from a 1cm/½in diameter yellow cane and press it against the head to form the bill.

4 Pack the gaps around the duck with wedges of blue clay to make a circular shape and wrap with a thin sheet to hold it together. Roll to consolidate the pieces and surround with a sheet of dark blue. Roll the cane to smooth the join and trim the concave ends.

Flower Cane

Choose colours that contrast strongly to give the design clarity. Slices are best cut using a tissue blade: chill the cane if necessary to avoid distorting the pattern.

Complex Canes

Rolling the canes under a small sheet of plexiglass reduces their size.

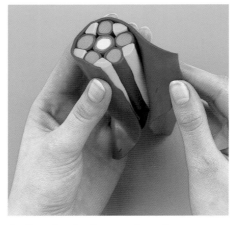

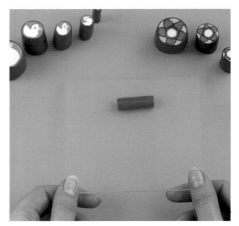

1 Roll one cane for the flower centre, five for the petals and two for the leaves, each about 2cm/¾in wide. Wrap the centre cane in a thin sheet of a contrasting colour, and the petals in a different colour. Roll the canes to smooth the seams.

2 Cut the leaf canes lengthways into quarters. Roll out a thin sheet of a new colour. Arrange the canes to form a flower and wrap the bundle in the prepared sheet. Roll the cane to compact it, and trim the ends.

To make canes of different diameters, stop rolling at each size required and cut the cane in half. Reserve one half and continue to roll the other. Different canes can be joined and rolled together to create complex designs.

Metallic Finishes

Polymer clay can be decorated by brushing on metallic powders, or metal leaf can be applied to a sheet of clay before it is shaped.

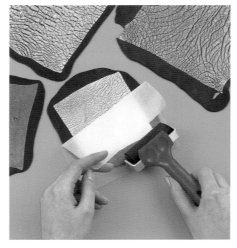

1 Lay a sheet of Dutch metal leaf, metal side down, over a sheet of clay. Roll over it with a brayer as you lay it down to exclude air bubbles. Rub all over the backing paper then gently and slowly peel it off.

2 For a crackle finish, cover the applied metal leaf with another piece of paper and roll a brayer over the paper until the required amount of cracking is achieved.

3 Any mould can be used to shape polymer clay or impress a texture in the surface. To gild a moulded piece, lightly brush the mould with metallic powder before embossing the clay.

Provided it is kept damp and soft when not in use, modelling clay is easy to handle and shape. Always keep spare clay covered with plastic wrap or in a plastic bag.

Modelling Clay Techniques

Preparing Clay

Knead the clay until it is soft and malleable and all air bubbles are eliminated. Colour can either be kneaded into the clay before modelling or painted on once the finished model has hardened.

Mixing Clay with Colour

Use a concentrated colouring agent such as paste food colouring, which will produce intense colours without making the clay too wet.

1 Add colour gradually to achieve the shade you want. Remember that the shade will change slightly when the clay dries out.

2 Roll the clay into a long sausage, fold over and repeat. Add more colour as necessary and repeat until the colour is evenly distributed.

Mixing Clay with Hardener

This treatment makes the clay more difficult to work with, so keep it in a plastic bag. You can soften it slightly by kneading in a little hand cream.

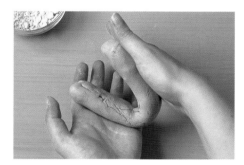

1 Make an indentation in the clay and add powder hardener. Fold the clay over the powder and knead a little before rolling into a sausage.

2 Fold the sausage over and add more hardener. Continue to knead until you have used all the powder you need.

Decorating Clay

A wide variety of decorative techniques, such as sponging and gilding, can be used on modelling clay.

Some types of self-hardening clay have a tendency to flake, so it is a good idea to seal the surface with one or two coats of diluted PVA (white) glue.

Apply paint to modelling clay with a brush or sponge, and spray or brush on a minimum of two coats of varnish.

Drying Clay

To avoid cracking, dry clay gradually, covering it with a damp cloth to slow the process.

Tape small, flat clay pieces to a board in order to prevent them from curling, adding a weight if necessary. Remove any rough edges when dry with some fine abrasive paper.

The main materials used in mosaic are the individual pieces, known as tesserae, which can be ceramic, glass, china or any solid material. The other important material to consider is the base, which should be rigid.

Mosaic Materials

Adhesives

There are several ways of attaching tesserae to a background. Cement-based tile adhesive is the most well-known, and it can also be used to grout between the tesserae once the design is complete. For a wood base, use PVA (white) glue. For a glass base, use a silicone-based or a clear, all-purpose adhesive; to stick glass to metal, use epoxy resin. PVA is also used to prime a wooden base to make a suitable surface for the mosaic.

Admix

This is added to tile adhesive for extra adhesion.

Bases

Mosaic can be made on top of almost any rigid and pre-treated surface. One of the most popular bases is plywood.

Brown paper

This is used as backing for mosaics created by the semi-indirect method. Use the heaviest available.

Grout

Specialist grouts are smoother than tile adhesive and are available in a variety of colours.

Shellac

Use this to seal finished mosaics, especially those for outside use.

Tesserae

Mosaic material is described as tesserae.
Ceramic tiles – These are available in a range of colours and textures, glazed or unglazed. Household tiles can be broken to size using a hammer, or cut with tile nippers for precise shapes.
China – Old china makes unusual tesserae. It creates an uneven surface, so is suitable for decorative projects rather than flat, functional surfaces. Break up china using a hammer.
Marble – Marble can be bought pre-cut into small squares; to cut it with accuracy you need specialist tools.
Mirror glass – Shards of mirror add a reflective sparkle to a mosaic. Mirror can be cut with tile nippers or glass cutters, or broken with a hammer.
Smalti – This is opaque glass that has been cut into regular chunks. It has a softly reflective surface.
Vitreous glass tesserae – These are glass squares which are corrugated on the back to accommodate tile adhesive. They are hardwearing and thus perfect for outdoor projects.

Many of the tools needed to make mosaics are ordinary household equipment; the rest can be purchased in a good hardware store. A pair of tile nippers is the main piece of specialist equipment you will need.

Mosaic Equipment

Abrasive paper

Use coarse-grade paper to prepare wood. To clean finished mosaics, use fine-grade paper and wear a mask.

Clamps or bench vice

These are needed when cutting out the wooden base for projects.

Dilute hydrochloric acid

Use to clean cement-based grout from the finished mosaic if necessary. Always wear protective clothing, and work in a well-ventilated area.

Drill

A hand electric drill is needed for hanging projects on the wall.

Glass cutter

Use to cut or score glass tesserae.

Paint scraper

This is used to remove awkward pieces of dried tile adhesive or grout from the surface of a completed mosaic.

Protective face mask

Wear a mask when mixing powdered grout, sanding the finished mosaic, and cleaning with hydrochloric acid.

Protective goggles

Wear safety goggles when you cut or smash tiles, and when working with hydrochloric acid.

Sacking (heavy cloth)

Use to wrap up tiles before breaking them with a hammer.

Saw

Use to cut wood (choose a hacksaw for basic shapes, and a jigsaw for more complex ones).

Spatula/Spreader/Squeegee

Used for spreading glue or other smooth adhesives, such as cellulose filler, on to your base material.

Tile nippers

These are invaluable for cutting shaped tiles, especially curves.

You may also find all or some of the following items extremely useful: bradawl (awl), chalk, craft (utility) knife, flexible knife, rubber (latex) gloves, hammer, felt-tipped pen, masking tape, mixing container, nailbrush, paintbrushes, pencil, plastic spray bottle, pliers, ruler, scissors, set square, sponge, tape measure.

Covering small objects, including trinket boxes and jewellery items, with mosaic is an ideal way to recycle favourite pieces of china that get broken. Plan the whole design before you glue any pieces down.

Mosaic Techniques

Cutting Tesserae

If specific shapes are not required you can use a hammer, but tile nippers will cut regular tesserae and shape small pieces of china accurately.

Using Patterned Ceramics

Plain china can simply be broken up into the sizes you need, but if you are breaking up patterned china there may be areas of the pattern, such as flowers or birds, that you want to use as features in your mosaic. Break up the china around the pattern you want to keep, then "nibble" the edges with tile nippers to achieve the right shape while keeping the motif central.

1 Break up large tiles and pieces of china by hitting them with a hammer. Remember to wear goggles to protect your eyes. It is safer to wrap each piece of ceramic in a thick cloth to prevent flying shards.

2 To cut regular shapes, hold tesserae in the tips of tile nippers and squeeze the handles together. The piece should break along the line of impact. Create a specific shape by nibbling small fragments off the edges.

Applying Mosaic

Three-dimensional objects need to be covered in mosaic using the direct method, in which the tesserae are cemented face up on the surface. Plan the design by laying the pieces in position on a flat surface before starting to apply the adhesive.

1 Cover the surface with adhesive and press the tesserae into it. Cover with grout, taking care to fill the gaps between the tiles. Remove the excess grout, leave to dry, then clean.

2 If you are following a design drawn on the base, apply a thin layer of tile adhesive to the wrong side of each piece and stick it in place.

3 If the tesserae are reflective, such as mirror glass or gold or silver smalti, try placing them at slightly different angles on a three-dimensional surface, to catch the light.

Grouting   Mosaics are grouted primarily to give them extra strength and a smoother finished surface. The process has the added bonus of tying the tesserae together and making the mosaic look complete. Some mosaics are left ungrouted: this is usual when smalti are used, as the ungrouted surface is considered more expressive.

Grouts come in the form of powder, which has to be mixed with water to a workable consistency, or ready-mixed, which is usually more convenient for small projects. On flat surfaces, a squeegee can be used to spread the grout over the surface and push it between the crevices.

1 When grouting three-dimensional mosaics or uneven surfaces, it is easiest if you first spread the grout over the surface with a flexible knife.

2 Wearing rubber gloves, use your fingers to rub the grout well into the mosaic, pressing it into every single one of the crevices and making sure as you do so that there are no air bubbles or empty spaces. Use a sponge or wet cloth to wipe away the excess grout immediately and fill in any gaps if necessary.

3 When grouting flat areas of mosaic, an alternative method is to spread the grout while it is in powder form. Use a powdered cement-based adhesive and spoon it on to the surface, then spread it with a soft brush, working it into the spaces between the tiles.

4 When all the crevices are filled, spray the mosaic with water using a household plant mister. Make sure enough water is sprayed and absorbed into the cement to set it completely. You will probably need to repeat the grouting process, as the cement will shrink when it is wetted.

Cleaning

It is advisable to get rid of as much excess grout as you possibly can while it is still wet. You will find that most purpose-made grouts can be scrubbed from the surface using a stiff-bristled brush, such as a nailbrush, and then polished off. Cement mortars and cement-based adhesives need rougher treatment to remove any excess thoroughly, and you will probably need to use sandpaper.

A quicker alternative is to dilute hydrochloric acid and paint it on to the surface to dissolve the excess cement. Remember that this process should be done outside, as it gives off toxic fumes. When the excess cement has fizzed away, wash off the residue of acid from the mosaic with plenty of water.

Glass in a variety of colours and textures is available from specialist stained glass suppliers, together with glass paints, self-adhesive foil and other materials, some of which may also be found in craft stores.

Glassworking Materials

Contour paste

This creates raised lines on glass to act as a barrier for glass paints.

Copper foil

Wrap this tape around the edges of glass so panes can be soldered together.

Borax-based flux (auflux)

This is brushed on to clean metal while soldering and to make solder flow well.

Glass

Clear picture glass can be used to make small boxes and panels. Stained glass is made in many colours and different effects. Small pieces of mirror add extra sparkle.

Glass nuggets

Widely available in many different colours and sizes, glass nuggets can be glued on to decorate glass and other surfaces. They combine effectively with glass paints.

Glue

Two-part epoxy resin glue takes a few minutes to harden, which gives you some time to position the elements of a piece. Ultra-violet glue hardens in daylight, but is not suitable for gluing red glass as the colour blocks ultra-violet rays.

Solder

Various different formulations of metal alloys are currently manufactured for use as solder. When working with glass, solder is used to join panels framed in copper foil, and 50:50 tin and lead is best for this purpose, as it flows easily.

Wire

Copper wire is ideal for use with foiled glass panes as it is compatible with tin solder. It can be used for making loops and hooks, or for decoration. Silver jewellery wire can be used as a decorative binding.

Working with glass does require some specialist equipment, all of which can be purchased from glass suppliers. You will probably already have many of the other items you need.

Glassworking Equipment

Craft (utility) knife

A craft knife will cut through lead and copper foil.

Fid

This tapered wooden tool is used for pressing down copper foil and self-adhesive lead.

Flux brush

This is used to paint borax-based flux (auflux) on to copper foil.

Glass cutter

A glass cutter has a hardened metal wheel that is run over the glass to score it. The glass can then be broken along the scored line.

Gloves

Wear gloves to protect your hands from glass splinters and toxic lead.

Goggles

It is always essential to wear goggles when working with glass.

Lint-free cloth

Use clean, dry rags to polish glass.

Pliers

Grozing pliers are used to take off any sharp shards of glass. Round-nosed (snub-nosed) and square-nosed pliers are useful for straightening and curling wire and bending sharp angles.

Scythe stone

Otherwise known as a glass file, a cigar-shaped scythe stone is used to file down the sharp or jagged edges left after glass has been cut. Use this tool on every piece of glass you cut before doing any further work on it.

Soldering iron

You will need a 75-watt (or higher) soldering iron, and a stand to support it when it is hot.

Wire cutters

Use these to cut wire neatly.

Practise scoring and cutting spare pieces of plain picture glass before you try it on more expensive stained or etched glass. Always smooth all the cut edges and dispose of waste glass with care.

Glassworking Techniques

Cutting Glass Once the glass has been scored, there are various different ways of breaking it along the line. Try each of the methods illustrated below to see which one works best for you.

1 Hold the glass cutter with your index finger on top and your thumb and second finger gripping each side, with the grozing teeth facing towards your elbow. When you are cutting correctly, with the cutter at right angles to the glass, this position will give you a lot of movement in your arm.

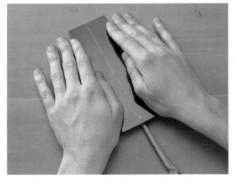

2 Always cut glass from edge to edge, one cut at a time. Start with the cutter at right angles to the glass and draw it with a consistent pressure from one edge to the other.

3 Now you can break it along the scored line. The first method is to hold the cutter upside down between thumb and first finger, holding it loosely so that you can swing it to hit the underside of the line with the ball on the end. Tap along the line following the crack. The glass will break off.

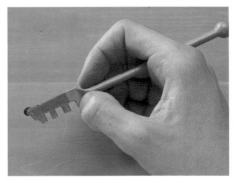

4 The second method is to hold the glass with your hands on each side of one end of the scored line. Apply firm pressure, pulling down and away from the crack. This works only if the score mark is very straight.

5 The third method is to lay the cutter on the work surface and place the glass on top with the scored line over the cutter.

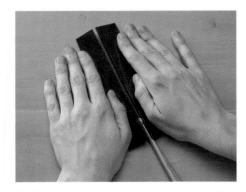

6 Put pressure on both sides of the line with the bases of your thumbs. Push down until the glass breaks.

Foiling Glass

Self-adhesive copper foil has a protective backing paper which you should remove just as you are applying the foil to the glass. Try not to touch the adhesive as any grease or dust will stop it sticking.

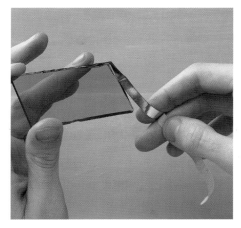

1 With the piece of glass in one hand, hold the foil between the fingers of your other hand and use your thumb to peel back the backing paper as you work around the edges of the glass.

2 Stick the foil to the edges of the glass all the way around, and overlap the ends by 1cm/½in.

3 Using two fingertips, press the foil down on to both sides of the glass all the way around. Use a fid to flatten the foil on to the glass to make sure it is firmly stuck.

Soldering Glass

Foiling the edges of glass panes allows you to join them by soldering the metal. It's a good idea to tack together all the elements of a design with a blob of solder on each joint so that you can make any adjustments before completing the soldering.

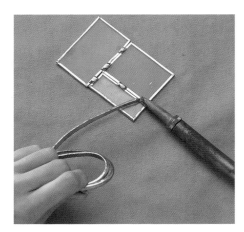

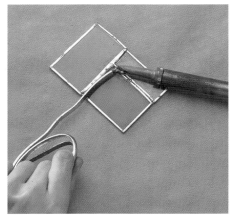

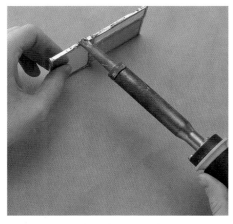

1 Apply flux to all the copper foil showing on the first side. With the hot soldering iron in one hand and the solder in the other, with about 10cm/4in uncoiled, tack the pieces together by melting a blob of solder on to each adjoining edge.

2 To complete the joint, melt the solder and allow it to run along the copper. Do not let it go too flat but aim to build up an evenly rounded seam, which is stronger and looks neater. Turn the piece over and flux and solder the other side of the joint.

3 Tin the edges by first fluxing, then running the soldering iron along each edge. There is usually already enough solder on the edge to spread around.

An easy-to-make clay mould is used to model these eye-catching silver earrings, so it's easy to produce as many pairs as you want – you can make them as gifts for everyone who admires them on you!

Moulded Star Earrings

you will need

self-hardening modelling clay

rolling pin

tracing paper, pencil, paper or thin card (stock) and scissors (for template)

modelling tools

pair of earring studs

bonding adhesive

black acrylic paint

paintbrushes

silver powder

varnish

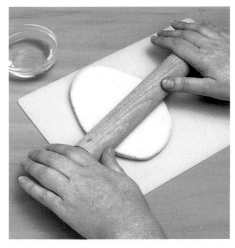

1 Roll out a small piece of clay to a thickness of 8mm/⅜in.

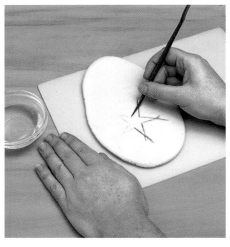

2 Trace the template from the back of the book on to thin card or paper. Cut the star shape out of the clay.

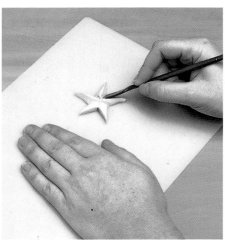

3 Mark a line from the centre of the star to each point where two rays meet and use the flat side of the modelling tool to mould each point to a 90° angle. Smooth the star with water, tuck the edges in neatly and leave to dry.

4 Take a small ball of clay and press with your palm until it is about 2cm/¾in thick. Press in the hardened clay star then lift out carefully without distorting the mould. Leave to dry.

5 Use the mould to make further clay stars. Lift them out of the mould and place face up on the work surface. Trim off the excess clay with a modelling tool. Allow to harden.

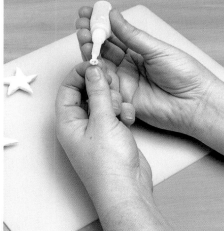

6 Glue an earring stud to the back of each star.

7 Paint the stars with black acrylic paint and leave to dry completely.

8 Mix silver powder with varnish and brush this over the stars to complete.

Brighten up a child's coat (or your own) with these friendly spiders. Use self-cover buttons, matching the size to your buttonholes, and snap the fronts on to the backs before you start to decorate them.

Spider Buttons

you will need

polymer clay: bright green,
black and white

self-cover metal buttons

rolling pin

craft (utility) knife

self-healing cutting mat

gloss acrylic varnish

paintbrush

1 Roll the green clay out thinly and cut out a circle large enough to cover one of the buttons. Mould the clay over the button.

2 Using black clay, roll very thin strands for the legs and press them on to the button. Roll a finer strand for the spider's thread.

3 Roll a pea-sized ball of black clay and press it into the centre of the button for the spider's body.

4 Create eyes from two balls of white clay and two tiny balls of black clay. Bake in a low oven following the clay manufacturer's instructions. Apply two coats of gloss varnish when cool.

These very striking earrings shimmer with a distressed black and gold paint effect that looks stunning but is actually quite simple to achieve. The faces are easily modelled out of clay.

Sun and Moon Earrings

you will need

modelling clay

rolling pin

jar lid

modelling tools

earring posts and butterfly backs

strong clear glue

fine-grade abrasive paper

black acrylic paint

artist's brushes

gold powder

matt (flat) acrylic varnish

1 Roll out two pieces of clay, each to a circle about 5mm/¼in thick and 7.5cm/3in in diameter. Use a jar lid as a template to mark an inner circle. With a modelling tool, build up the central area so it is higher than the outer area but still flat.

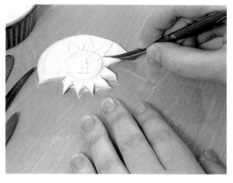

2 Model the features of your sun on the raised central area with a modelling tool. Mark the rays around the face and cut away the excess clay. Pierce some dots in the face and rays and leave to dry for 1–2 days. Model a moon in the same way.

3 Glue the earring posts in position. Sand between the rays for a smoother look. Paint black. Mix the gold powder with the varnish, then paint. With a semi-dry brush, go over the face up and down quickly, so that the black underneath shows through and accentuates the features of the face. Paint the moon in the same way.

Formalized leaves and gilded scroll-work turn simple square boxes into encrusted Renaissance-style treasures. You could line the inside of each little box with sumptuous fabric to hold small pieces of jewellery.

Florentine Boxes

you will need

square and rectangular cardboard craft boxes

tracing paper

hard and soft pencils

masking tape

modelling clay

modelling tools

PVA (white) glue

medium and fine artist's brushes

acrylic craft paints: white, pale lilac and pale blue

dark and pale gold metallic paint

matt (flat) acrylic spray varnish

1 Enlarge the templates provided to fit the top and sides of the box lid. Trace the outline with a hard pencil, then rub over the reverse with a soft pencil. Tape the paper to the lid. Draw over the lines again using a hard pencil to transfer the design.

2 Make the four leaf shapes from small rolls of modelling clay and press them into position on the box lid. Use modelling tools to add the details, and smooth the clay with a damp finger.

3 Make the dots from small balls of clay. Press them in place with the point of a pencil.

4 Finish the design on top of the lid by adding the four trefoil motifs on the corners.

5 Make the scrolls and leaves for each side of the lid. Allow the clay to dry thoroughly. ▶

6 Paint the lid with PVA glue diluted with an equal quantity of water. When the glue is dry, paint the lid and box with white acrylic paint.

7 Now paint the lid of your box with a base coat of pale lilac.

8 Add a stippling of pale blue paint, applied with an almost dry brush.

9 Using a fine brush, paint the motifs in dark gold. When dry, add pale gold highlights as desired.

10 Give a textured look to the lid by brushing lightly over the surface with a dry brush loaded with a small amount of gold paint.

11 Paint the bottom of the box to match, adding a small amount of gold paint to each edge. Finish with a protective coat of matt varnish.

These jolly earrings, made using the cane technique, will suit the mood of a hot summer's day or cheer up a dull one. Have fun making the orange slices as realistic as you can – these even have pips.

Orange-slice Earrings

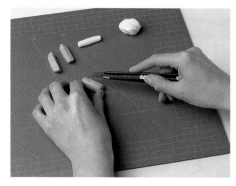

you will need

polymer clay: pearl, pale orange and dark orange

rolling pin

craft (utility) knife

self-healing cutting mat

bamboo skewer

cheese grater

2 eye pins

round-nosed (snub-nosed) pliers

2 large rings

2 earring hooks

1 Roll a 5mm/¼in diameter sausage of pearl clay. Roll the pale orange clay into a short 1.5cm/⅝in diameter sausage and cut it lengthwise into four triangular segments.

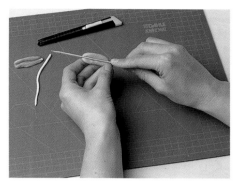

2 Cut lengthwise into two of the triangles and insert a skewer. Press the clay together to form a tunnel. Fill the tunnel with the sausage of pearl clay and reform the triangular shape.

3 Roll out a piece of dark orange clay thinly and cut strips 1cm/½in wide to fit between the segments. Arrange the pieces together to make a half cylinder. Roll out a 3mm/⅛in layer of pearl and a 2mm/¹⁄₁₂in layer of dark orange for the peel and mould these around the curved side of the cylinder.

4 Make two 1cm/½in balls in dark orange and roll on a cheese grater to make them look like small oranges. Fit an eye pin through the centre of each. Trim any overlapping edges from the half cylinder and roll the peel on a grater.

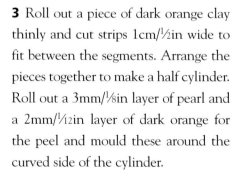

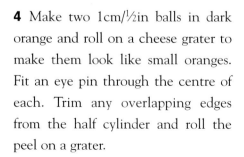

▲ **5** Cut two 5mm/¼in slices from the cylinder and make a hole in each for a ring. Bake the pieces following the clay manufacturer's instructions. To assemble each earring: using round-nosed pliers, loop the wire extending from the eye pin in each small orange and snip off any excess. Put a large ring through the orange slice and attach to the loop below the small orange. Attach the earring hook to the loop above the small orange.

Glow-in-the-dark polymer clay covered with silver leaf is embossed with spiral patterns to create an intriguing effect on this hair slide (barrette). In the dark, a subtle glow emanates from tiny cracks in the silver leaf.

Abstract Hair Clasp

you will need

½ block glow-in-the-dark
polymer clay

rolling pin

pencil, thin card (stock) and
scissors (for template)

craft (utility) knife

silver leaf

brayer

old jewellery or buttons

dark blue bronze powder

artist's brush

hair slide (barrette) clip

varnish

epoxy resin glue

1 Roll out some polymer clay to a thickness of 3mm/⅛in. Draw the shape required on card, and cut this template out. Place the card on the clay and cut round it with a craft knife.

2 Apply silver leaf to the clay shape. Roll over the backing sheet with a brayer until the leaf has adhered, then gently peel off the backing.

3 Create a regular pattern around the edge of the silvered clay by pressing interestingly shaped jewellery or buttons into it to leave indentations.

4 Fill in the central area with a random pattern applied in the same way as in step 3 but using different shapes if you wish.

5 Lightly brush the surface around the edge with dark blue bronze powder.

◄ **6** Slip a small piece of thin card through the full width of the hair slide clip then place the clay shape on top. The clay will mould itself to the curved shape of the slide but the card will prevent it sagging too much. Bake in this position, following the clay manufacturer's instructions. When cool, varnish the surface and glue the clip on to the back.

Polymer clay simplifies the craft of jewellery-making because stones can simply be pushed into the clay. Metal leaf and powders readily adhere to the surface of unbaked clay to give it a lustrous richness.

Burnished Bronze Necklace

you will need

1 block black polymer clay

rolling pin

craft (utility) knife

bronze powders: various colours

artist's brush

leaf pastry cutter

modelling tool

jewellery wire

wire cutters

glass cabochon stones

varnish

round-nosed (snub-nosed) pliers

glass beads

necklace clasp

1 Roll out a piece of black clay, about 4mm/³/₁₆in thick, and cut in half. Dust lines of bronze powders in various colours on to the surface of one piece.

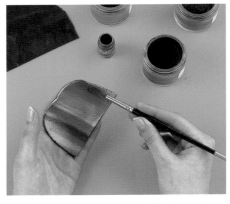

2 Now carefully mark vertical lines between the colours and then cut out leaf shapes in such a way that your vertical lines form the leaf's central veins. Create the smaller veins on the leaves by using a modelling tool.

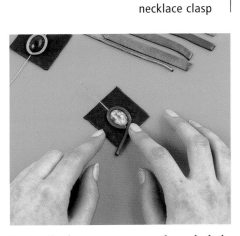

3 Roll the remaining clay slightly thinner and cut it into five or six 5cm/2in squares. Place a length of jewellery wire centrally on each square and place a cabochon stone over it. Cut strips 3mm/⅛in wide from the remaining bronzed clay and wrap these round each stone, cutting off the excess.

4 Arrange three leaves to one side of the stone. The wire should consistently project from the same side of the middle leaf on each square, to allow the necklace to hang in a tight-fitting curve when assembled.

5 Press the leaves and stone surround gently but firmly enough to meld them together and to hold the stone securely in place. Cut out the black clay around the shape using a craft knife and smooth along the joins at the sides to obliterate them. Bake following the manufacturer's instructions.

6 Carefully varnish the bronzed areas and allow to dry. Using round-nosed pliers, make loops in the wire ends and trim off the excess wire. Hook the pieces together and close up the hooks. Attach glass beads at each end of the necklace in the same way to achieve the correct length. Finally, wire on a clasp.

It's hard to believe that this exotic-looking piece of jewellery is made from a piece of plastic pipe covered in polymer clay. Gold leaf and embedded stones help to effect a magical transformation.

Egyptian Bangle

you will need

4cm/1½in length of plastic drainpipe

1 block black polymer clay

rolling pin

Dutch gold leaf

brayer

craft (utility) knife and ruler

self-healing cutting mat

smoothing tool

modelling tool

gemstones

epoxy resin glue

acrylic craft paints

fine artist's brush

gloss acrylic varnish

1 Roll out a strip of clay large enough to cover the section of plastic pipe. Apply the gold leaf and crackle the surface using a brayer (see Polymer Clay Techniques).

2 Cut the clay exactly to size and wrap it carefully round the pipe, making sure there are no air bubbles.

3 Join the clay, taking care not to rub off any gold leaf when smoothing over the seam where the ends meet.

4 Using a modelling tool, mark a faint line around the circumference 1cm/½in from one edge. Measure the circumference, divide the figure by the number of stones you wish to use and mark their positions along the line. Press the stones into the clay.

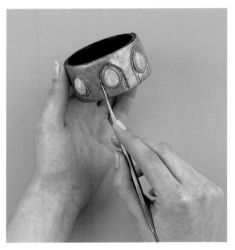

5 Draw a line round each stone then impress an arch around it.

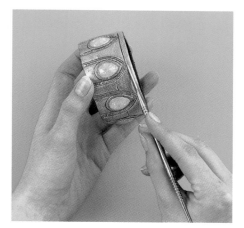

6 Draw a line around the bangle joining the tops of the arches.

7 Etch a narrow petal shape between the arches all round the bangle to form the centre of the stylized flower.

8 Draw a pointed petal on either side of the central one then add smaller petals in between.

9 Carefully remove the stones and bake the bangle following the clay manufacturer's instructions. When cool, glue the stones back in place.

10 Paint the flowers and background sections in colours of your choice. Finish with several coats of gloss varnish to protect the paint and gilding.

The tiers of these glamorous but lightweight earrings swing when you move and glitter as they catch the light. Gold leaf scrolls, gemstones and droplet beads all contribute to the opulent effect.

Shimmering Earrings

you will need

jewellery wire

ruler

wire cutters

round-nosed (snub-nosed) pliers

½ block black polymer clay

rolling pin

craft (utility) knife

Dutch gold leaf

brayer

gemstones: oval 1cm/½in long;

rectangular 1.5cm/⅝in long;

round 5mm/¼in diameter

dressmaker's pins

palette knife (metal spatula)

eyelet or similarly shaped object

smoothing tool

gloss acrylic varnish

paintbrush

large clip-on earring backs

epoxy resin glue

10 droplet beads

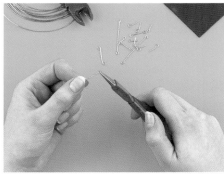

1 Cut 12 x 2cm/¾in wire lengths; form a loop in one end of each. Cut two 3cm/1¼in lengths and two 6cm/2½in; loop all ends. Roll out the clay, cut in two and gild one half. Cut backing sheets from ungilded clay: two 3cm/1¼in squares (for the top tiers); two 4 x 3cm/1½ x 1¼in oblongs (central tiers); two 1.5cm/⅝in squares (bottom tiers).

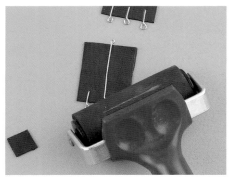

2 Lay three short wires along the bottom of each middle-sized backing sheet and press them in with the brayer. Lay a long wire down the centre of each large backing sheet with a short, single-hooked wire on either side, and press in. Lay the remaining short, single-looped wires one on each of the small backing sheets and press in.

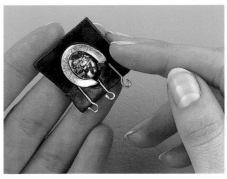

3 Press an oval stone on to each of the middle-sized backing sheets. Cut two strips 3mm/⅛in wide from the gilded clay and wrap securely round each stone, trimming off any excess. Add more strips to decorate.

4 Cut two 3cm/1¼in lengths of gilded clay. Pinch both ends to taper, shape into scrolls and press on to the mid-sized backing sheets to cover the wires. Cut two small squares of gilded clay, cut in half diagonally and place above the scrolls. Press decorative marks and lines around the border with a pin. Trim off the excess backing sheet. ▶

5 Press the square stones centrally on the two large backing sheets. Cut a 1.5cm/⅝in square and a 1cm/½in square from gilded clay, then cut across to make four triangles. Press a large triangle above each stone and a small one beneath. Cut four thin strips of gilded clay to fit on each side of the stones.

6 Using a palette knife, press in all the pieces to make a tight fit round the stones (avoid distorting the shapes). Cut two thin strips 4.5cm/1¾in long from the gilded clay, curl them into scrolls and place one under each bottom triangle. Use an eyelet to stamp a circular design on the top triangles.

7 Make six tiny beads, roll them in gold leaf and use them to decorate the tops of the middle tiers. Trim off the excess backing sheet.

8 Place one of the remaining stones on each of the small backing squares. Cut two strips of gilded clay 3cm/1¼in long and wrap them round the stones. Trim off the excess backing sheet.

9 Using a smoothing tool or your finger go round the edges of each piece to make sure all the surfaces are melded together. Bake following the manufacturer's instructions and allow to cool.

10 Varnish all the gold leaf surfaces and allow to dry. Glue the clip-on earring backs to the backs of the first tier.

11 Join all the tiers of the earrings together, using round-nosed pliers to close up the wire hooks.

12 Hang droplet beads from the free hooks, closing up the hooks. The droplets at the bottom can be slightly bigger than the others.

Once you have mastered the art of making millefiori canes (see Polymer Clay Techniques), you can use them in some exciting ways. Here, slices from different canes are applied to partially baked polymer clay beads.

Composite Beads

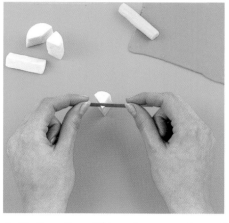

1 Roll a 3cm/1¼in diameter log of white clay. Cut it into five wedges from the centre and slice off the sharp angle of each wedge. Roll out a 6cm/2½in yellow cane and a flat sheet of green clay.

2 Arrange the white triangular wedges, separated by 3mm/⅛in slivers of green, around the central yellow cane to form a flower. Roll, using a sheet of Plexiglass to smooth.

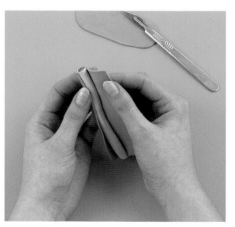

3 Make a jelly roll with 4 x 10cm/1½ x 4in strips of yellow and fluorescent orange clay (see Polymer Clay Techniques). Wrap it in a sheet of pale blue clay about 1mm/¹⁄₁₆in thick.

4 Reduce the picture cane to a diameter of 1cm/½in and the flower cane and jelly roll to about 5mm/¼in (see Polymer Clay Techniques). Reserve the trimmings to make beads. Cut the jelly roll into 7.5cm/3in lengths. Cut a 7.5cm/3in length from the duck cane. ▶

5 Cut the flower cane into four lengths of 7.5cm/3in. Arrange them in a cross pattern around the picture cane, interspersed with four lengths of jelly roll cane.

6 Roll the assembled canes carefully between your hands to meld them together then wrap in a 3mm/⅛in thick sheet of green clay.

7 Cut the cane in half using a tissue blade, rocking while you cut to avoid distorting the picture. Wrap one of the halves in a 3mm/⅛in thick sheet of coral clay, cut off the surplus and roll under Plexiglass to smooth the sides.

8 Make up several compilation canes then reduce them further to different sizes. Shave off thin slices to cover the surface of previously prepared disc beads and roll them smooth. It is a good idea to make the canes and the beads compatible sizes.

9 Use some of the surplus picture and flower cane to make borders or sides for the beads. Press them on firmly so they will adhere, then smooth over.

10 Cover previously prepared round beads, filling any triangular shaped gaps with slices of the surplus small flower or picture cane. If you cover any bead holes, pierce through again after you have rolled the surface smooth. Bake all the beads following the clay manufacturer's instructions.

The delicate mosaic covering this trinket box is made entirely from old cups and plates. The finished box is ideal for displaying on a dressing table, and can be used to store jewellery and other small treasures.

Floral Trinket Box

you will need
wooden box
PVA (white) glue
old household paintbrush
bradawl (awl) or other sharp instrument
soft dark pencil
white and patterned old china
tile nippers
cement-based tile adhesive
admix
flexible knife
cloths
paint scraper

1 Prime the top and sides of the wooden box with diluted PVA glue. Leave to dry, then score the surface with a bradawl or other sharp implement to provide a key.

2 Using a soft pencil and the template at the back of the book, draw a grid on the box. Draw a flower in each square, with a large flower in the centre.

3 Cut the pieces of white china into small squares. Mix the tile adhesive with admix. Using a flexible knife, spread this along the grid lines, a small area at a time.

4 Press the white tesserae into the adhesive in neat, close-fitting rows. Cover all of the grid lines on the top and sides of the box. Leave overnight for the adhesive to dry completely.

5 Using tile nippers, cut out small pieces of the patterned china. Sort them into colours. Position the tesserae on the box and plan the colour scheme.

 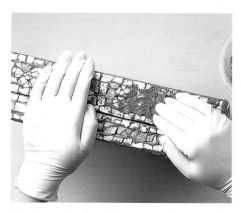 

6 Spread the tile adhesive, strengthened with admix, over each section of the top and sides in turn. Press in the tesserae to make each flower and fill in the background. Leave to dry.

7 Spread tile adhesive all over the surface of the mosaic, working it right into all the crevices with your fingers. Wipe the excess adhesive off the mosaic with a damp cloth.

8 Using a flexible knife, smooth the tile adhesive around the hinges and clasp, if there is one. Remove any excess adhesive immediately with a cloth before it dries. Leave to dry.

9 Use a paint scraper to scrape off any tile adhesive that may have dried on the surface of the mosaic. Take care not to scratch the surface of the tiles.

10 When all of the excess grout has been removed, polish the surface of the box with a soft cloth, making sure that you rub each tile fragment to a high shine.

The threatening face on this Aztec-inspired box symbolizes magical protection for the treasures inside, while the colours evoke precious materials found on Aztec artefacts, such as turquoise, coral and gold.

Aztec Jewel Box

you will need

wooden box with hinged lid

felt-tipped pen or soft pencil

glass globules backed with gold and silver leaf

PVA (white) glue

masking tape

fine artist's brush

vitreous glass mosaic tiles

tile nippers

Cinca ceramic tiles

sand

cement

black cement dye

squeegee

sponge

soft cloth

plastic bag

1 Draw the design on the box with a felt-tipped pen or soft pencil. Here, the teeth and jaws of the beast are drawn immediately below the opening edge of the lid.

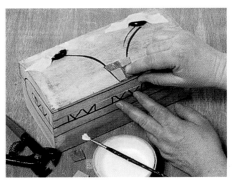

2 Stick on glass globules for the eyes, holding in place with masking tape until dry. Cut vitreous glass tiles in coral for the nose and lips and pink and terracotta to line the lips. Use a fine brush to glue small pieces.

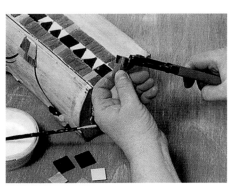

3 Cut black and white tesserae into precise triangular shapes to fit the areas marked for the teeth, then glue them in position.

4 Cut tesserae in shades of turquoise, blue and green into wedge shapes, and use them to tile around the eye sockets and to delineate the snout. Cover the sides of the box, cutting tiles where necessary to fit. Include a few small glass globules positioned randomly. When tiling around the hinges, leave about 1cm/½in untiled so that the box can be opened easily. Leave to dry, then complete the lid in the same way.

5 Mix three parts sand with one part cement and add a little black cement dye. Add water a little at a time until the desired consistency is attained. Rub the cement on to the surface of the box. Scrape off the excess cement with a squeegee, then rub the box with a slightly damp sponge. Finish by polishing with a dry cloth, then cover the box with a plastic bag so that it will dry as slowly as possible.

This quirky little box makes a bold romantic statement. To break the mirror, wrap it in newspaper and hit it with a hammer, then carefully pick out fragments of the shape and size you need to cover the lid.

Mirrored Trinket Box

you will need

section of poster tube

cardboard

pencil

scissors

masking tape

pair of compasses

PVA (white) glue

newspaper

4 marbles

artist's brushes

epoxy resin glue

chemical metal filler (car-body

repair filler)

mirror fragments

white acrylic primer

gouache paints

gloss acrylic varnish

gold enamel paint

1 Stand the section of tube on a sheet of cardboard and draw round it. Cut out the disc and tape to the tube. Cut out a slightly larger circle for the lid and another 1cm/½in smaller in diameter. Glue the two together. Bend a roll of newspaper into a heart shape and attach to the lid with masking tape. Cover four marbles with tape.

2 Tear some newspaper into strips and brush with PVA glue diluted with water. Cover the box, lid and marbles with several layers of papier mâché. Leave to dry thoroughly. Glue the marbles to the box base using epoxy resin glue. Mix up the filler, spread it over the lid, and carefully push in the mirror fragments.

3 Paint the whole box, except the mirror pieces, with PVA glue. When dry, prime the box with white acrylic primer. Paint the design with gouache.

4 Coat the painted box with several layers of gloss acrylic varnish, and leave to dry. To finish, pick out details of the design in gold enamel.

This delicate little glass box is ideal for storing small pieces of jewellery such as earrings, and makes a pretty ornament. Opal glass, available from stained glass specialists, adds an extra-special lustre.

Opal Glass Box

you will need

tracing paper (and perhaps ordinary paper) and pencil (for template)

carbon paper

blue opal glass

clear 2mm/¹⁄₁₆in picture glass

cutting square or straight-edge

glass cutter

cutting oil

scythe stone

mirrored blue stained glass

4mm/³⁄₁₆in and 6mm/¹⁄₄in copper foil

fid

borax-based flux (auflux) and flux brush

soldering iron

50/50 tin-lead solder

tinned copper wire

wire cutters

permanent black felt-tipped pen

round-nosed (snub-nosed) pliers

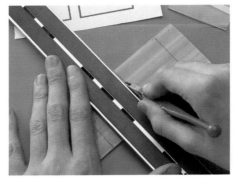

1 Trace the template provided for this project at the back of the book, enlarging to the size required. Transfer the shapes to the glass using carbon paper. Using a cutting square or a thick straight-edge, score and break the side pieces of the box from clear glass and blue glass. Transfer the octagonal base outline on to the mirrored blue glass. Score and break the glass. Smooth all the edges with a scythe stone dampened with a little water.

2 Wrap the blue side pieces in 6mm/¹⁄₄in copper foil and the thinner clear picture glass in 4mm/³⁄₁₆in foil. Press the foil down firmly using a fid.

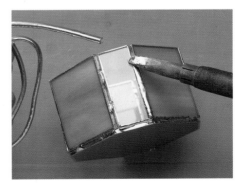

3 Apply 4mm/³⁄₁₆in copper foil around the top surface of the mirror base to ensure that the sides bond securely. Wrap the sides using 6mm/¹⁄₄in copper foil. Press down firmly with a fid.

4 Brush all the copper-wrapped pieces with flux and lightly tack-solder the side pieces into place around the base of the box, adjusting them slightly to fit together if necessary.

5 Reflux and solder all copper surfaces. For a neat finish, run a bead of solder to fill the point where the side sections meet. Wash thoroughly to remove any traces of flux.

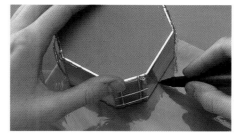

6 With the box balanced on one side, hold the end of a piece of wire just overlapping one of the clear glass sections. Brush with flux and touch the tip of the iron to the wire to solder it. Trim off the other end with wire cutters and repeat, applying two vertical wires over the clear glass panel.

7 Solder two horizontal pieces of wire to the pair of verticals. Solder them on oversize, then trim them to length when they are soldered in place. Wash thoroughly to remove any traces of flux. Repeat steps 6 and 7 to decorate the other clear glass panes.

8 Lay the glass for the lid face down and place the box upside down over it. Trace around the box with an indelible black pen. Score and break the glass just inside the lines. Smooth with a scythe stone and wrap the edges of the lid with 6mm/¼in foil. Apply flux and plate the foil with solder.

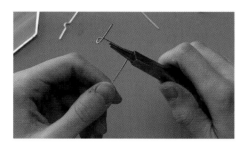

9 Cut two pieces of wire about 10cm/4in long. Using the template as a guide, bend two kinks in one piece using a pair of round-nosed pliers. Bend two right angles in the other piece of wire to coincide with the kinks in the first. Bend the two ends into loops and trim off the excess wire with wire cutters.

10 Apply flux to both pieces of wire. Solder the kinked section to the box and the looped section to the lid. Wash thoroughly to remove any traces of flux. Slot the lid hinge section into the body section to complete the box.

Templates

Patterns for some of the projects are given here so you can make templates. The way you copy these may depend on the materials being used, but cutting out a card template and drawing round it is often the best approach.

Tracing

Unless you have access to a photo-copier, you will need to trace the printed pattern before transferring it to a piece of card for cutting out.

1 Use a pen or pencil to draw over the image. Turn the tracing over on a piece of scrap paper and use a soft pencil to rub over the lines.

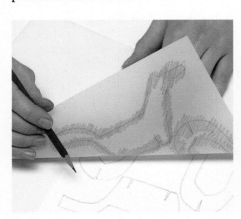

3 Lift off the tracing to reveal the design. Go over the lines if necessary before cutting out the template.

2 Place the tracing, right side up, on a sheet of paper or card (stock). Using a hard pencil, draw firmly over all the lines of the design.

4 When working with fabric, it may be possible to trace the design directly using a fabric pen. Tape the drawing to a light box or window and tape the fabric over it to hold it still while you draw.

Scaling up

You may want to make a template that is larger than the printed design. Scaling up is easily done using a photo-copier with an enlarging facil-ity, but failing this you can use graph paper. For very small designs, scaling down may be required.

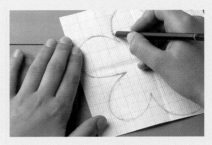

1 Trace the design and tape the tracing over a sheet of graph paper. Using an appropriate scale, draw the design on a second piece of graph paper, copying the shape from each small square to each larger square.

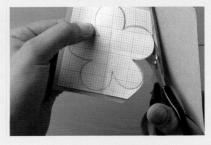

2 Lay or paste the graph paper template on a sheet of card and cut around the outline.

Fabric and Leather Templates

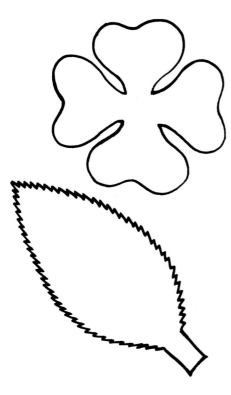

Felt Flower Brooch, p24

Floral
Headband
and Brooch,
p47

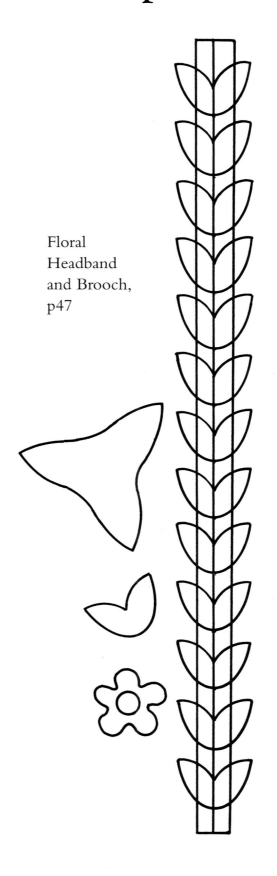

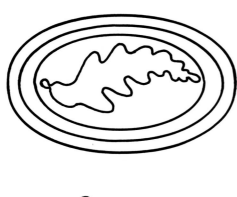

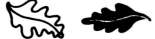

Oak-leaf Hair Clasp and Buttons, p48

Machine Embroidery Templates

Heart Hatpin, p58

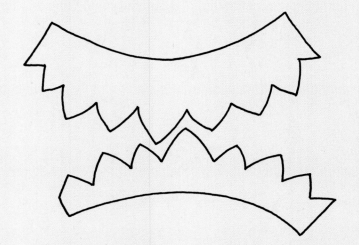

Glittering Hair Comb, p70

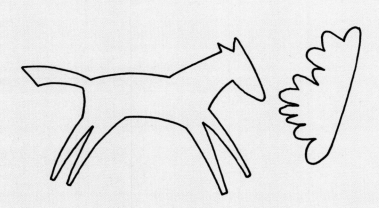

Horse Brooch, p63

Iridescent Earrings and
Pendant, p74

Beads and Shells Templates

Pearl Tiara, p92

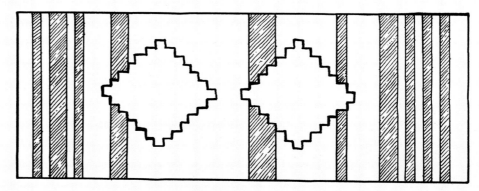

Woven Bracelet, p102

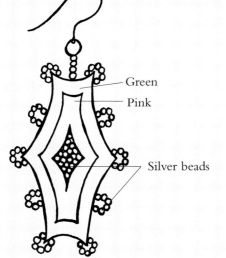

Green

Pink

Silver beads

Victorian
Earrings and
Brooch, p104

Fill in background with small beads

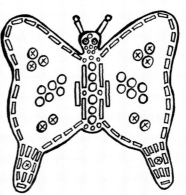

Beads marked with a cross are
black iridescent beads; all others
are plain black beads

Butterfly Brooch, p106

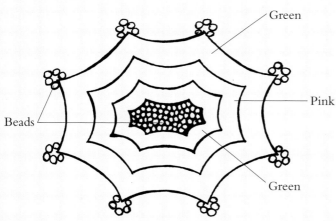

Green

Pink

Beads

Green

Enamelling and Metalwork Templates

Bird Lapel Pin, p124

Fishy Cufflinks, p140

Banded Ring, p138

Two alternative designs are shown here

Stargazer Earrings, p142

Pet Brooch, p144

Flower Pendant, p146

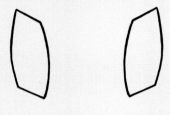

Shield Earrings, p148

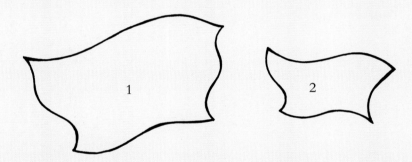

Wave Brooch, p151

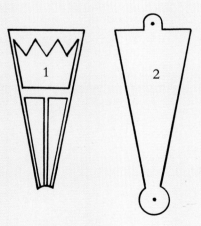

Triangular Pendant, p159

Cloisonné Earrings, p154

Paper, Card and Wood Templates

Fruity Bracelet, p180

Sun and Moon
Badges, p191

Winged Cupid Brooch, p186

Shooting Star Badge, p194

Crab Jewel Box, p196

Clay, Mosaics and Glass Templates

Moulded Star Earrings, p214

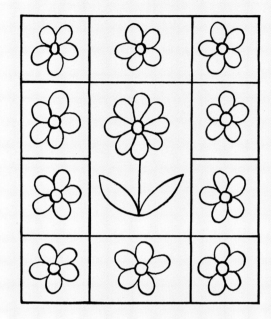

Floral Trinket Box, p234

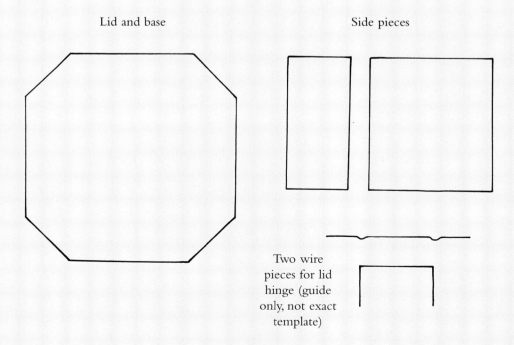

Lid and base

Side pieces

Two wire pieces for lid hinge (guide only, not exact template)

Florentine Boxes, p218

Opal Glass Box, p240

Index

A

acids 114, 116, 207
acorn buttons 28–9
adhesives
    beadwork 79
    claywork 200
    glassworking 210
    leatherwork 18
    metalwork 120
    mosaic 206
    paper and card 172
    ragwork 16, 17
    ribbonwork 13
    shellwork 81
    woodwork 177
appliqué 54
Aztec box 236–7

B

backings 16, 17, 52
badges 60–1, 191–5
baking parchment 201
balance earrings 84
bamboo mat 11
bead loom 78, 82, 102–3
beads 77, 78–9, 81, 100
    clay 202, 231–3
    enamel 128–9, 133–5
    felt 12, 20–1, 28–9
    glass 10, 36, 78, 200

gold foil 128–9
pre-strung 82
ribbon 30–1
rolled-paper 184–5
beadwork 78–9, 82–106
    bracelets 90–1, 102–3
    brooches 104–5, 106
    buttons 96–9
    cord beading 79, 90–1
    couching 82
    earrings 84, 100–1, 104–5
    embroidery 52, 104–5
    hatpins 85
    materials/equipment 78–9

necklaces 72–3, 86–7, 94–5
    techniques 82–3
    threading loom 82
    tiara, pearl 92–3
    trinket box 88–9
    Victorian 104–6
    woven 78, 82–3, 102–3
    wrapped 100–1
beeswax 18, 79
bird lapel pin 124–5
blackberry buttons 96–7
blazer badge 60–1
blender 173
bows, ribbon 13, 15
boxes 7, 201
    beadwork 88–9
    decoupage 188–90
    Florentine 218–20
    mosaic 234–7
    opal glass 240–1
    presentation 182–3
    sea-shell 108
    tinware 168–9
    wooden 196–7
bracelets
    bead 78, 90–1
    Egyptian bangle 226–7
    felt 22–3
    fruity 180–1
    harlequin 66–7
bradawl 177, 207

brass brush 115, 116
brass shim 62, 120, 168
brayer 201
bronze powder 200, 204
brooches 16
    beadwork 104–6
    cloisonné 157–8
    floral 24–5, 47
    horse 63–5
    painted tin 164–5
    pet 144–5
    ragwork 44–5
    ribbon rose 14
    spider's web 166–7
    star-sign 179
    starfish 56
    wave 151–3
    winged cupid 186–7
    wrapped wire 42–3
brown paper 206
butterfly brooch 106
buttons
    acorn, felt 28–9
    beaded 96–9
    multicoloured 126–7
    oak-leaf 48–9
    self-cover 79, 97–8, 200
    snail-shell 107
    spider 216

C
calico 52
card *see* paper
carders 11
ceramic fibre 114
Chinese necklace 94–5
claywork 200–5
  bangle 226–7
  beads 202, 231–3
  boxes 218–20
  buttons, spider 216
  cane work 203–4, 221,
    231–3
  colouring 202, 205
  drying 205
  earrings 214–15, 217,
    221, 228–30

equipment 201
hair clasp 222–3
materials 200
metallic finishes 204
modelling clay 200,
  201, 205
necklace 223–5
polymer clay 200, 201,
  202–4
preparing clay 202, 205
techniques 202–5
cloisonné 114, 154–61
cockle-shell necklace 109
coils, wire 122
contour paste 210
copper 114, 116
cord beading 79, 90–1

cotton fabric 16
cotton spheres 79, 96
couching 48, 55, 82
crab jewel box 196–7
crimp beads 20
crochet 84
crochet hook 16
cufflinks, fish 140–1
cutting mat 18, 173

D
darning foot 52
decoupage 172, 173
  box, roses 188–90
  techniques 175–6
  tinting prints 175
  varnishing 176
diamond earrings 68–9
domino hairslide and
  earrings 38–9
dressmaking shears 11, 16
drill 81, 83, 177, 207
dyes 10, 12, 19

E
earrings 7
  balance, beaded 84
  cloisonné 154–5
  diamond-shaped 68–9
  domino 38–9
  iridescent 74–5
  marbled felt 26–7
  orange-slice 221
  plique-à-jour 136–7
  ragwork 16, 38–9
  shield 149–50
  shimmering 228–30
  star 214–15
  stargazer 142–3
  sun and moon 217
  Victorian 104–5
  wrapped 42–3, 100–1
Egyptian bangle 226–7
embroidery 10, 52, 104
  ribbon 13, 15
  stitches 15, 55
  see also machine
    embroidery
embroidery hoop 16, 52, 53
enamel 114

enamel gum 114, 118
enamelling 114–19, 124–61
  beads 128–9, 133–5
  brooches 144–5, 151–3,
    157–8
  buttons 126–7
  cloisonné 154–61
  cufflinks, fish 140–1
  earrings 136–7, 142–3,
    149–50, 154–5
  equipment 115
  etching 117, 138–47
  finishing 119
  frosted finish 133
  kiln firing 119
  lapel pin, bird 124–5
  materials 114
  necklaces 128–9, 133–5
  pendants 146–7, 159–61
  plique-à-jour 136–7
  rings 130–2, 138–9
  soldering 116
  techniques 116–19

F
fabric paints 60, 79
fabric stiffener 10, 26
face masks 81, 83, 207
felt 10, 56
  backing 16, 17, 52
felt mop 115, 119
felteen 10, 26
feltwork 10–12, 20–9
  balls/beads 12, 26–7
  bracelet 22–3
  brooch, flower 24–5

clasps 48–9, 222–3
slides 14, 32–3, 38–41
hammer 121, 207
hardeners 200, 205
harlequin bracelet
66–7
hatpins 101
beadwork 85
embroidered 58–9, 62
heart hatpin 58–9
hessian 16–17
hooking 16, 17
horse brooch 63–5

buttons, acorn 28–9
earrings, marbled
26–7
equipment 11
materials 10
necklace, bead 20–1
techniques 12
fid 211
file 81, 115, 121, 123
filigree 58–9, 74–5
findings 7, 10, 16
fish cufflinks 140–1
fittings 7
flowers 182
beaded buttons 97
clay cane 204, 232
enamel 146–7
felt 24–5
leatherwork 47
mosaic 234–5
pipe-cleaner 163
wire-edged ribbon 13
flux brush 211
foil 114, 128, 172
copper 210, 213
gold foil beads
128–9
plastic 16, 44–5
frame saw 177, 178
fruity bracelet 180–1

G
gift wrap 172
gilding 200
glass 210
cutting 212
foiling 213
soldering 213

glass beads 10, 36, 78
glass cutter 207, 211
glass fibre brush 115, 119
glass nuggets 210
glass paints 88–9, 210
glassworking
boxes 238–41
equipment 211
materials 210
techniques 212–13
gloves 211
glue gun 13, 79, 81,
177
goggles 81, 83, 207,
211
grouting 206, 209

H
hair ornaments 106
combs 70–1, 92–3
bands 34, 47, 78
bobbles 40–1

I
inks 81
interfacing/interlining
52, 54, 60
iron 52

J
jewel boxes
Aztec, mosiac 236–7
Florentine 218–20
opal glass 240–1
seashell 108
tinware 168–9
wooden, crab 196–7
jewelled buttons 98
jump rings 128

K
kaolin 114
kiln firing 115, 119

L
lapel pin 124–5
leather 18
leatherwork 18–19,
47–9
dyeing 19
floral 47
materials/equipment
18
moulding 19
oak-leaf 48–9
punching 19
techniques 19
linen thread 18
locket, shell (Valentine's)
110–11

M
machine embroidery
50–75
bracelet 66–7
brooches 56–7, 63–5
earrings 68–9, 74–5
free-standing 52
hair comb 70–1
hatpins 58–9, 62
materials/equipment
52
necklace 72–3
pendant 74–5
pressing 52
techniques 53–5
matting salts 133
metal beads 78–9
metal sheet 62, 114
working with 123
metallic leaf 200, 204
metalwork 7, 120–3

brooch, tin 164–5
equipment 121
jewel box, tin
168–9
materials 120
sun hatpin 62
techniques 123
mica 114
mirrored trinket box
238–9
modelling tools 201
mosaic
boxes 234–7
cleaning 209
cutting tesserae 208
equipment 207
grouting 209
materials 206
techniques 208–9

N
necklaces 7
beaded cord 72–3
beading 83
bronzed 224–5
Chinese 94–5
cockle-shell 109
felt bead 20–1
furry flower 163
pompom 46
striped 133–5
Venetian 86–7
needles 11, 18
beading 52, 78
machine 52, 53

O
oak-leaf hair clasp and
buttons 48–9
orange-slice earrings 221
oven 201
oxalic acid 19

P
paint
acrylic 108, 172, 177,
200
enamel 120, 164, 172
fabric paints 60, 79
glass paints 88–9, 210
gouache 172
paintbrushes 115, 173,
177, 201, 207
palettes 79, 118
paper and card 172–6,
179–90
beads, rolled 184–5

box 182–3
corrugated card 108,
172, 182
equipment 173
materials 172
techniques 174–6
see also decoupage;
papier mâché
paper clips 120
papier mâché
bracelet, fruit
180–1
brooches 179,
186–7
making 174
materials/equipment
172, 173
mirrored box 238–9
pulp 172, 174
pasta machine 201
pastry cutters/moulds
201
pearl tiara 92–3
pendants 94
flower 146–7
iridescent 74–5
metal blanks 7
triangular 159–61
pestle and mortar 115,
117
pet brooch 144–5
photo-etching 117,
138–47
pinking shears 18
pipe cleaners 120, 163
plastic 16, 40, 44–5
plexiglass 201
pliers 79, 121, 122, 207,
211
plique-à-jour 114, 136–7
plywood 177, 206
pocket clips 162
polishing 83, 119
pompom necklace 46
presser foot 52
pressing 52
primer 172, 177
protective clothing
121, 123, 211
pumice powder 114,
119
punch 18, 19, 121
putty, reusable 81, 83

R
ragwork 16–17, 38–46
backing/finishing 17
brooches 42, 44–5
earrings 39, 42
hair accessories 38–41
hooking 17
materials/equipment 16
necklace, pompom 46
ring 44–5
techniques 17
wrapped jewellery
42–3
reptilian ring 130–2
resists 114
ribbons 13, 100
embroidery 13, 15
paper 182
pleated 35–8, 110
for shellwork 81, 110
streamers 13, 85
types 13
velvet 100
ribbonwork 13–14, 30–7
bows 13, 15
embroidery 13, 15
materials 13
necklace 30–1
roses 14, 32–3, 34, 85
techniques 14–15
trinket bag 35–8
rings
banded 138–9
plastic foil 44
reptilian 130–2
rolling mill 115, 149, 151
rolling pin 201

roses, ribbon 13, 14
    hair accessories 32–4
    hatpins 85
    leaves 14, 34
ruler 173, 207

S
saws 177, 178, 207
scaling up 54, 242
scissors 11, 16, 18,
    79, 173, 207
scythe stone 211
seashell box 108
set square 177, 207
sewing machine 52, 53
shellac 81, 172, 206
shells 77, 80–1
    drilling 81, 83
    polishing 83
    sanding 81, 83
shellwork 80–3, 107–11
    buttons 107

jewellery box 108
locket 110–11
materials/equipment
    80–1
necklace 109
techniques 83
shield earrings 149–50
shooting star badge 194–5
sieves 115, 118
silver 114, 116
snail-shell buttons 107
soap flakes 11
solder 114, 120, 210
soldering 115, 116
    glass 213
soldering iron 121, 211
spider buttons 216
spider's web brooch 166–7
sponge 173, 207
stain, leather 18
star earrings 214–15
star-sign brooch 179
starfish brooch 56–7

stargazer earrings 142–3
stopping-out varnish 114, 117
sun and moon
    badges 191
    earrings 217
sun hatpin 62
sunflower badge 192–3

T
tape, florist's 14
tassel buttons 98
templates 242–9
    scaling up 54, 242
    tracing 242
tesserae 206, 208
thread
    beading 78, 82
    double 55
    embroidery 16, 18,
      42, 52
    invisible 52
    metallic 10, 52, 55,
      100–1
    polyester 29
    sewing 10, 18
tiara, pearl 92–3
tile nippers 207
tin plate 120, 123
    brooch 164
    jewel box 168
tin snips 121, 123
tinting prints 175
tongs 115
tracing 242
triangular pendant 159–61
trinket bag 35–8
trinket boxes
    beaded 88–9
    decoupage 188–90
    floral mosaic 234–5
    mirrored 238–9
tweezers 79, 81, 115

V
Valentine's locket 110–11
varnish 172, 177, 200
    crackle 172, 176, 190
    decoupage 176
Venetian necklace 86–7
vice 21, 123, 207
Victorian-style 104–6

W
wallpaper paste 172
washing soda 114
water-soluble film 52, 54
wave brooch 151–3
weddings 32–3, 92–3
winged cupid brooch 186–7
wire 13, 16, 114
    beading 78, 84
    copper 120, 210
    cutting 13
    florist's 13, 14, 15
    galvanized 120, 162
    gold 100–1
    jewellery 200, 210
    nylon-coated 10
    wrapped 42–3
wire cutters 13, 121, 211
wire-edged ribbon 13, 14
wired tape 120
wirework
    brooch 166–7
    coils 122
    equipment 121
    materials 120
    pocket clips 162
    techniques 122
    twisting wire 122
woodworking 177–8
    badges 191–5
    box, crab 196–7
    frame saw, using 178
    materials/equipment
      177
    smoothing surfaces 178
    techniques 178
wool, felting 10–12
wrapped jewellery 42–3,
    100–1

Acknowledgements

The publishers would like to thank the following craftspeople for designing the projects in this book. Apologies to any people who may, unintentionally, not be credited.

Ofer Acoo:
Spider's Web Brooch p166, Moulded Star Earrings p214, Sun and Moon Earrings p217

Helen Baird:
Floral Trinket Box p234, Aztec Jewel Box p236

Evelyn Bennett:
Tinware Jewel Box p168

Victoria Brown:
Felt Bead Necklace p20, Felt Bracelet p22, Felt Flower Brooch p24, Marbled Earrings p26, Acorn Buttons p28, Pearl Tiara p92

Louise Brownlow:
Iridescent Earrings and Pendant p74, Beaded Balance Earrings p84

Judy Clayton:
Ribbon Beads p30, Embroidered Sun Hatpin p62, Wrapped Earrings p100

Marion Elliot:
Painted Tin Brooches p164, Rolled-paper Beads p184

Sophie Embleton:
Fruity Bracelet p180

Lucinda Ganderton:
Rose Hair Accessory p32, Ribbon Rose Hairband p34, Ornate Beaded Hatpins p85, Venetian Necklace p86, Florentine Boxes p218

Dawn Giullas:
Pocket Clips p162

Jill Hancock:
Sun and Moon Badges p191, Sunflower Badge p192, Shooting Star Badge p194

Alison Harper:
Victorian Earrings and Brooch p104

Angela Harrison:
Wrapped Jewellery p42

Susie Johns:
Glittering Trinket Box p88

Julie Johnson:
Pompom Necklace p46

Kitchen Table Studios:
Egyptian Bangle p226

Mary Maguire:
Floral Headband and Brooch p47, Oak-leaf Hair Clasp and Buttons p48, Snail-shell Buttons p107, Cockle-shell Necklace p109, Valentine's Locket p110, Furry Flower Necklace p163, Spider Buttons p216, Abstract Hair Clasp p222, Burnished Bronze Necklace p224, Shimmering Earrings p228, Composite Beads p231

Abigail Mill:
Sparkling Starfish Brooch p56

Jane Moore:
Banded Ring p138, Fishy Cufflinks p140, Stargazer Earrings p142, Pet Brooch p144, Flower Pendant p146

Deirdre O'Malley:
Opal Glass Box p240

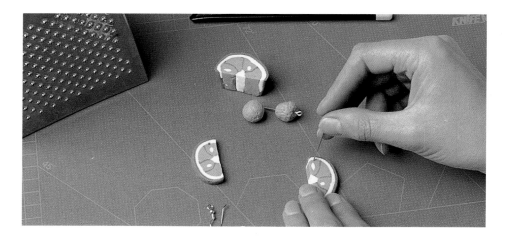

Denise Palmer:
Plique-à-jour Earrings p136

Maggie Pryce:
Decoupage Roses Box p188

Alex Raphael:
Multicoloured Buttons p126

Lizzie Reakes:
Domino Hairslide & Earrings
p38, Hooked Hair Accessories
p40, Crispy Brooch & Ring p44

Kim Rowley:
Star-sign Brooch p179, Winged
Cupid Brooch p186, Mirrored
Trinket Box p238

Ruth Rushby:
Bird Lapel Pin p124, Gold Foil
Beads p128, Cloisonné Earrings
p154, Cloisonné Brooch p156,
Triangular Pendant p159

Isabel Stanley:
Trinket Bag p35, Heart Hatpin p58,
Blazer Badge p60, Horse Brooch p63,
Harlequin Bracelet p66, "Diamond"
Earrings p68, Glittering Hair Comb
p70, Beaded Necklace p72,
Cord-beaded Bracelet p90, Chinese
Necklace p94, Beaded Buttons p96,
Woven Bracelet p102

Sarah Wilson:
Reptilian Ring p130, Striped

Necklace p133, Shield Earrings p148,
Wave Brooch p151

Dorothy Wood: Butterfly Brooch
p106, Orange-slice Earrings p221

Photography
The publishers would like to thank
the following photographers for their
work on the featured projects:

Karl Adamson
Lisa Brown
Steve Dalton
Nicki Dowey
James Duncan
John Freeman
Michelle Garrett
Janine Hosegood
Tim Imrie
Gloria Nicol
Lizzie Orme
David Parmiter
Debbie Patterson
Debi Treloar
Peter Williams

Thanks also to the authors, stylists
and illustrators whose work is
featured in this book.

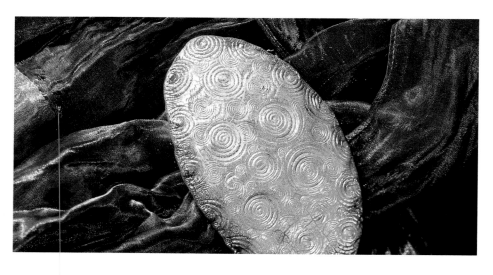